30 Meditations on the

Writings of C. S. Lewis

30 MEDITATIONS
ON THE WRITINGS *of*
C. S. LEWIS

PERRY BRAMLETT, RUEBEN P. JOB
NORMAN SHAWCHUCK

Abingdon Press / Nashville

30 MEDITATIONS ON THE
WRITINGS OF C. S. LEWIS

Library of Congress Control Number: 2019950765

ISBN 13: 978-1-5018-9836-5

20 21 22 23 24 25 26 27 28 29 — 10 9 8 7 6 5 4 3 2 1
MANUFACTURED IN THE UNITED STATES OF AMERICA

Contents

Contents

Introduction

Clive Staples Lewis was his full name, but all his friends called him Jack. He is one of the most trusted and read Christian authors of the past hundred years, and perhaps the most effective Christian apologist ("defender of the faith") of the twentieth century. Some call him the man who helped make Christianity intellectually respectable, the apostle to the skeptics, and a Christian for all people. Lewis may have influenced (and is still influencing) more people for the cause of Jesus Christ and his church than perhaps any modern Christian writer.

Lewis was an Irishman (born in Belfast) who lived most of his adult life in the university city of Oxford, England. He was a fairly large, red-nosed, rumpled, jolly man; one of his friends said that he looked like a "prosperous farmer." He had a booming laugh, a superb speaking voice, and a large measure of what we today call personal magnetism or charisma. Lewis was possibly the most famous Christian in the world from the middle 1940s until his death in 1963 (the same day that President

John F. Kennedy was assassinated in Dallas). And he still may be the most famous Christian in the world.

The author of thirty-eight books, including works of medieval history, literary criticism, and history that are still read today, Lewis was a prolific writer. He wrote Christian science fiction and fantasy, stories for children, and theology for the average educated person. His works explored love, temptation, miracles, suffering and grief, prayer, ethics, and the Bible. He once said that he talked about heaven in nearly all his books. He also told the story of his own conversion. He was a man of letters that are among the finest and most interesting ever written by anyone. Many of his books, both fiction and nonfiction, remain in print and many are best sellers. Some, like *Mere Christianity*, *The Screwtape Letters*, *The Chronicles of Narnia*, and *The Great Divorce*, have sold millions of copies worldwide and have been printed and reprinted in many languages.

And thanks to the numerous biographies and other volumes devoted to his life and works, there is more interest than ever in Lewis as a writer of devotional works and a defender of Christianity. The film *Shadowlands* helped focus even more attention on him as a real human being who loved and grieved and triumphed after a great loss. *A Grief Observed*, written after the death of his wife, Helen Joy, is widely acknowledged as a moving and poignant account of spiritual struggle and recovery.

Jack Lewis was one of those extraordinary Christians

who had, and still has, the remarkable ability to change lives. People from all over the world have testified how reading and listening to his works led them to faith or how his works helped their old faith "come alive" with renewed vigor and intellectual and spiritual integrity. People from diverse backgrounds, such as Eldridge Cleaver, Charles Colson, Sheldon Vanauken, and M. Scott Peck, have all called Lewis the primary Christian influence in their pilgrimages to an initial or a deeper faith. And he has been quoted by leaders like Pope John Paul II, Billy Graham, and six American presidents. Children's authors such as Madeleine L'Engle, Susan Cooper, and Katherine Paterson have drawn heavily on Lewis's books. Famous novelists like Walker Percy, Robertson Davies, and Tom Wolfe have used Lewis's ideas in their works. Many more admirers could be listed.

One reason for Lewis's success was his humility and lack of pretention. He never thought himself a great man, and he realized that the life of Christian faith always means starting over every day and "keeping on keeping on." This truth shines like a beacon in his works and helps the reader not only to identify with Lewis but also to trust him as a reliable guide who practiced what he wrote.

This book is an introduction to the spirituality of Jack Lewis, but it is also an encouragement to readers to understand and cultivate their own spirituality. It seems that "spirituality" has been defined by almost everyone, but at its core it is the idea of knowing God. This means not just knowing *about* God, but experiencing God to the full or drawing near to God. Authentic spirituality is at the heart of our Christian faith, transforms the way we actually live, and also has a lot to do with the authenticity in our life and thought. Spirituality that is authentic involves our personal ideas about the church and faith and our attitudes toward the world, culture, history, and more. It should be mentioned that authentic Christian spirituality should be based not on feelings (Lewis would concur), nor is it a vague idea of happiness. But it does have everything to do with who we are, what we do, how we think, and how we approach life; indeed, spirituality is a lived experience. Lived Christian spirituality is how Christian people deepen their experience of God and, in the words of Brother Lawrence, "practice the presence of God."

Many years ago, Francis de Sales wrote his now-famous *Introduction to the Devout Life*, which he called a "collection of bits of good advice" designed to help people "live an ordinary life." He said further that the Christian's "ordinary life" should be one that can live in the world "without being infected by any of its moods." One of the goals of authentic spirituality should be to free ourselves from the social, political, and economic "principalities and powers" of this world, and this takes a concentrated "effort of the spirit." Lewis's thought has a similar emphasis.

We hope that by reading this book, the reader will identify with Jack Lewis, a great Christian who carried his own salvation with fear and trembling, as it is said in Philippians 2:12. Lewis was a convert in the truest sense. Though baptized into the Church of Ireland, he lived outside the faith for many years before he first became a believer in God (a theist), then a committed disciple of Jesus Christ. He had kept his distance from the church for over two decades, and during this time he became friends and colleagues with materialists and unbelievers of all stripes. When he finally became a Christian, he knew firsthand what it was like to be immersed in non-Christian culture. He talked, argued, and thought his way to faith, and he understood the doubts, fears, and questions of the readers he hoped to reach. He asked their questions, spoke their language, understood their emptiness and frustrations, recognized their dissatisfaction with organized religion, and finally, he knew from experience what they were experiencing and what might awaken them.

A Guide to the Daily Office

An inquiring mind, an open heart, a command of language, and a persuasive writing may have been the combination of gifts that caught the attention of readers while C. S. Lewis was living, as it continues to do so today. We have tried to reflect each of these gifts in this volume, which is designed for all who seek to explore, understand, and enjoy the fruits of this gifted life. It is also our hope that the exploration of some of the central themes in Lewis's writing will offer opportunities to discover renewed faith and trust in God and greater integrity in daily witness.

The simple daily office that we suggest is a way of approaching each theme with prayer and reflection. Each chapter includes an excerpt from Lewis's work, an exploration of a theme in Lewis's thought, and a Scripture verse.

Lewis incorporated Bible reading, study, and prayer into his life. Since each of us is a unique individual and

God is infinite, it is natural that each of us develop a way of living that reflects our unique spirituality and our growing relationship with God. Therefore, the suggested daily office incorporates the wisdom of those who have gone before and allows flexibility for the individual user. We invite you, under the guidance of God's Spirit, to design and develop a life-giving rhythm of Bible reading, spiritual reading, prayer, reflection, and response that is appropriate for you and your setting. The daily office is one way to structure this practice.

Opening

Pray for the guidance of the Holy Spirit and your openness to God's prompting.

Spiritual Reading

Read the excerpt from C. S. Lewis's writings. Take time to listen for what Lewis may have in store for you. If you wish to go further, have a Lewis book at hand and read a paragraph or two to supplement the brief excerpt.

Scripture

The Scripture readings, which are included with each chapter, have been selected to shed light on the theme. Read the selection slowly and prayerfully and permit each passage to address you and the situation of the world. Remain open to insights that relate to your life.

Reflection

Read the opening essay and reflect on what the author said and what it evoked for you.

Record Your Insights

Journal about the discoveries, insights, and questions the readings prompted.

Prayer

Offer your prayers of thanksgiving, intercession, and petition.

Commitment to God

Conclude your time of prayer and reflection by deliberately placing your life into the care of God to be shaped, used, and sustained.

1

Salvation

Spiritual Reading

He came to this world and became a
man in order to spread to other men
the kind of life He has—by what I call
"good infection." Every Christian is
to become a little Christ. The whole
purpose of becoming a Christian is
simply nothing else.

Mere Christianity

On Salvation

Rueben Job

The doctrine of salvation "freely given" is perhaps the most difficult of the Christian doctrines for modern Americans to understand or appreciate. After all, part of the American mythos is the belief in individual agency, that people should pull themselves up by their own bootstraps and be the masters of their own fates. Indeed, it is the nature of humanity to claim we are the masters of our destiny, and it troubles us to think that there may be One outside ourselves who holds our fate in hands other than our own.

And yet, Christians affirm God's saving activity in Jesus Christ. God has done something for us in Christ that we could not do for ourselves.

The children of Israel experienced themselves as a collective people before God. As such, the salvation of each member of the tribe was contained within the community: their sins were corporate and the forgiveness God extended to them was dependent upon a corporate acceptance of God's proffered salvation. The salvation of the Israelites relied upon a shared apprehension of God's love for the entire world (John 3:16) and God's willingness to offer salvation not as a result of one's personal holiness but as a result of being found and claimed within the community of God's people.

We who live in the modern Western world cannot begin to appreciate such a posture. A proud and independent people, we desire to be strong, solitary beings. We like to believe that our salvation is the result of our own efforts and our own solitary encounter with God.

However, sooner or later we come to realize that it is quite impossible to save ourselves. It is equally impossible to be saved and to stay saved as a lone ranger making our way through life apart from God and the community of the redeemed.

For this reason, the author of Hebrews exhorted the early church not to stop meeting together with other believers (10:25). It is within the context of the community that salvation might be experienced and enjoyed. And salvation is a true gift, not earned but bestowed, and kept current in the memory of the congregation as it rehearses the gift most precious in regular worship and teaching. Salvation is free to all who choose to be saved and live in vital connection to God.

Christianity is concerned with forming human beings into new creatures, the kind that the apostle Paul referred to as sons and daughters of God. And this is

Scripture

*A man named Simeon was in Jerusalem. He was righteous
and devout. He eagerly anticipated the restoration of Israel,
and the Holy Spirit rested on him. The Holy Spirit revealed
to him that he wouldn't die before he had seen the Lord's
Christ. Led by the Spirit, he went into the temple area.
Meanwhile, Jesus' parents brought the child to the temple
so that they could do what was customary under the Law.
Simeon took Jesus in his arms and praised God. He said,*

> *"Now, master, let your servant go in peace
> according to your word,
> because my eyes have seen your salvation.
> You prepared this salvation in the presence of all
> peoples.
> It's a light for revelation to the Gentiles
> and a glory for your people Israel."*

Luke 2:25-32

the most shocking part of the salvation story: Jesus, the second person of the Godhead, died for us that we might be saved from the consequences of our sins and receive our full inheritance as children of God.

Of this, C. S. Lewis says in *Mere Christianity*, the most shocking aspect of Christianity may be its assertion that by giving our lives to God, we become the sons and daughters of God. Surely it must mean something else!

Lewis was an atheist for much of his youth and young adulthood. Raised in a nominally Christian home, Lewis became angry with God when his prayers for the healing of his ill mother were not answered as he wished; she died an early, painful death. Accordingly, Lewis rejected any idea of God and became a self-avowed atheist.

But God—"the Hound of Heaven," as the poet Francis Thompson says—pursued him. In October 1930, Lewis wrote to his friend Arthur Greeves that he had started attending morning chapel but that he thought that his faith had become mere talk. He hoped that somewhere within that was a tiny seed of true faith.

The following January, Lewis again wrote to Greeves, reporting that Lewis's brother, Warren, was beginning to believe in the claims of Christianity—even though he had resisted that view. Lewis expressed gratitude that he and his friends were at the same time becoming open to Christian faith. This led to his confessing his faith to Greeves in an October letter, wherein he said that he had moved from believing in God to definite belief in Christ.

Through these letters, Lewis introduces us to his conversion from atheism to Christianity. This was a change of life perspective that wrought not only conversion for Lewis and his brother, Warren, but also a salvation that brought rescue to countless people, as they heard, thought, read, and believed. For them, and for all who believe, salvation became full and complete.

2

Joy

Spiritual Reading

All joy (as distinct from mere pleasure,
still more amusement) emphasizes
our pilgrim status; always reminds,
beckons, awakens desire. Our best
havings are wantings.

A Mind Awake

On Joy

Perry Bramlett

There were really two C. S. Lewises. Alongside the clear-headed thinker there was another person: a person very much aware of the power of the imagination and the implications of this power for our understanding of reality. Perhaps the most original aspect of Lewis's writing is his appeal to the religious imagination. From a very early age he was conscious of deep human emotions that pointed to a dimension of our existence beyond space and time. These emotions stayed with Lewis throughout his adolescence and early manhood. He called these emotions (or feelings) "joy," and for many years he wondered to what they were pointing.

Joy, for Lewis, was a longing, a desire. He used several other words for "joy" in his writings, including *sehnsucht*, a German word for "romanticism," "desire," "sweet desire," and (in Lewis's words, after he became a Christian) "bright shoots of everlastingness." He used at least four images to describe joy, including distant hills, exotic gardens, islands, and music. In his autobiography, *Surprised by Joy*, Lewis tells of several experiences of joy from his childhood, and these experiences filled him with longing. Once, while standing near a flowering currant bush, he was seized with a desire for something he could not describe. This desire was a feeling that went far beyond the realm of "everyday experience." Another experience with joy came when he was reading *The Tale of Squirrel Nutkin*, by Beatrix Potter. Suddenly he was presented with the "idea of autumn," and it almost overwhelmed him. And once as a teenager he was reading a poem by Longfellow and was "instantly uplifted into huge regions of northern sky."

Lewis was fascinated with joy, and as time passed, he came to realize that joy was not nostalgia or a longing for the past like some people experience. Joy for Lewis went much deeper and farther. He called his quest for joy the central story of his life, and he distinguished it from happiness or pleasure in that anyone who has experienced joy will want it again, and it is always a desire for something "longer ago" or still "about to be."

As he came closer to Christian faith, Lewis began to understand what it was that aroused joy in him. He rejected the idea that his desire was psychological in origin (Freudian thought was sweeping Oxford at the time) and slowly came to see that these unquenchable longings were "arrows shot from the bow of God." And he discovered that joy was the "serious business of heaven."

Later, the mature Lewis addressed the question

Scripture

The angel said, "Don't be afraid! Look! I bring good news to you—wonderful, joyous news for all people. Your savior is born today in David's city. He is Christ the Lord. This is a sign for you: you will find a newborn baby wrapped snugly and lying in a manger." Suddenly a great assembly of the heavenly forces was with the angel praising God. They said, "Glory to God in heaven, and on earth peace among those whom he favors."

Luke 2:10-14

of joy in his sermon "The Weight of Glory," which he preached at the University Church of St. Mary the Virgin in Oxford, June 8, 1941. In this famous sermon he spoke of "a desire which no natural happiness could satisfy." This desire, he said, points *through* natural happiness and pushes people toward its real goal, of fulfillment in God himself. Lewis learned that joy had not been a physical, emotional, or psychological appetite. It had been a spiritual hunger that spilled over into his consciousness. He finally saw joy as what some would call our longing for heaven, and he knew that longing had been placed in him by God. After his conversion, Lewis often experienced stabs of joy, but he stopped thinking about it so much and just waited on and trusted God.

How is joy important to our own understanding of spirituality? Joy, as described by Lewis and others, is the culmination of the idea that there exists in us a desire that nothing in time and space, that nothing in earth, and that no created being can satisfy. The only thing that can ultimately satisfy us exists outside of time, space, and earth, and we call this God or heaven. One author noted that even if we recognize that our unsatisfied desires come from God ("the tug of the transcendent"), they can be "spent and misspent on indulgent emotionalism." It would be a dangerous thing to confuse joy with feelings or emotional desires, because we become slaves to the desire, the emotion itself. Joy points us toward God, and emotions and feelings, as Lewis said, will betray us if we put our trust in them and "turn into dumb idols, breaking the hearts of their worshippers," as he says in "The Weight of Glory." And we should realize that as beings created by God, we carry God's image, and our desires and feelings are clues that will lead us, hopefully, to a greater appreciation of God and finally to God.

3

Serenity

Spiritual Reading

The thing I am speaking of is not
experience. You have experienced only
the want of it. The thing itself has
never actually been embodied in any
thought, or image, or emotion. Always
it has summoned you out of yourself.
And if you will not go out of yourself
to follow it, if you sit down to brood
on the desire and attempt to cherish it,
the desire itself will evade you.

The Problem of Pain

On Serenity

Perry Bramlett

Lewis wrote in *Mere Christianity* that everyone, if they could honestly look into their hearts, would know that they want something that cannot be gained in and from this world. We all want a "settled satisfaction" (also called serenity) that is deeper and goes further than mere happiness. Many things seem, especially on the surface, to promise that settled satisfaction, but none can.

And he wrote further that there are usually three ways that people deal with this acute want—two wrong ways and one right way. One wrong way is the "fool's way," in which a person tries to sample everything on this earth in order to "catch the mysterious something." The problem eventually becomes these things themselves. We try new jobs, different partners, new homes, different hobbies and passions, and new types of learning, hoping that they will quench our thirst for ultimate satisfaction. And they all work, at least for a while.

Another wrong way is the "disillusioned sensible man"

approach, in which a person decides that it is all nonsense and then represses his desires and does not honestly deal with them. This person decides that any talk about ultimate fulfillment is just idealism and wishful thinking, and if a person uses common sense these ideas will soon vanish and not be so bothersome.

Lewis noted that his inner quest for settled satisfaction began to dominate his life. Yet he found that when he deliberately sought joy in poetry, music, or nature, nothing would happen. An event that changed his life was his finding a copy of George MacDonald's *Phantastes* in a railway bookshop. This famous work is a fairy-tale adventure in which MacDonald gives the sense of the "holiness of the ordinary"; that is, all experiences and all meaning comes from God. (Lewis was to later say that *Phantastes* baptized his imagination.)

According to Lewis, the right way is the Christian way, in which a person realizes or is taught that all of our desires exist because satisfaction for them must exist. We are hungry; there is food. Ducks want to swim; there are ponds. We get drowsy; there is sleep. Because we respond to melody and harmony, there is music and poetry. Lewis knew that all earthly desires are not satisfied, as when the duck is eaten by a predator before she can swim. But he believed that though Christianity tells us that not everyone will experience God and heaven, some will. And the great truth for him, and for us, is that if our desire cannot be satisfied on this earth, it can be satisfied somewhere else. If

Scripture

The LORD is my shepherd.
I lack nothing.
He lets me rest in grassy meadows;
he leads me to restful waters;
he keeps me alive.
He guides me in proper paths
for the sake of his good name.

Psalm 23:1-3

bodily pleasures, power, artistic achievement and appreciation, ambition, nostalgia, and other earthly appetites leave us ultimately empty, then we can only be truly satisfied by something not of *this* world.

Perceiving God in worship, where we may experience gratitude, is also a characteristic of serenity. A person may experience in worship a taste of this satisfaction of our deep longings. And worship inspired in Lewis a sense of gratitude. *Gratitude* is a word that we do not encounter often in the various definitions and discussions of worship. We hear the words *praise*, *preaching*, *liturgy*, *fellowship*, *prayer*, and others, and these are all worthy and constitute parts of a real worship experience. But gratitude, and being grateful, may be at the heart of what worship is all about. Gratitude lays bare the basic direction of our lives and our ambitions. When we worship in community, we come to the Creator; and with our fellow worshipers, we obey, give thanks, and are grateful. We worship a God who is a God of love, grace, and salvation. Can we give God anything less than our gratitude?

A few years ago, a pastor traveled to Oxford with the planned purpose of experiencing C. S. Lewis's city and heritage. This pastor wanted to have an experience of joy or desire like Lewis did. He thought that if he retraced Lewis's footsteps and visited his homes and schools and churches, he would have an encounter (of some kind) with God. He did not. He said later that he had forgotten what Lewis had written: that when one deliberately tries to plan or experience joy, nothing happens. Serenity cannot be grasped. We can, however, practice stillness, gratitude. Someone wrote that Lewis finally learned to know God because he had a childlike heart and that he, over time, learned to wait on God, to trust God, and to celebrate God when God showed himself. That would be a very good thing for all of us to do.

4

Prayer

Spiritual Reading

God is not hurried along in the
Time-stream of this universe any more
than an author is hurried along in
the imaginary time of his own novel.
He has infinite attention to spare for
each one of us. He does not have to
deal with us in the mass. You are as
much alone with Him as if you were
the only being He had ever created.
When Christ died, He died for you
individually just as much as if you had
been the only man in the world.

Mere Christianity

On Prayer

Norman Shawchuck

Prayer is somewhat of a quandary for me. I must constantly discipline myself to pray daily, whether I like it or not. It seems to me that I pray best in North Dakota. I am a creature of the prairie and its harsh climates. Each morning at seven I climb the creaky stairway in our one hundred-year-old house to my little sanctuary wrapped around by books, artifacts, and many precious memories. Always God is there, waiting, murmuring, "What took you so long?" I sense that our meeting time is as important to God as it is to me.

If there is anything we might learn of God in the Scriptures it is this: God desires our company, and God takes the initiative: God comes! I know this; yet my heart is often divided. I desire to be with God, yet I feel bound to my work; and so I say, "I will pray tomorrow." As I listen to the stories of my students and those I direct, I am aware that those who come for spiritual direction come for help for their prayer life.

In my discipline of evening prayer, I walk the stairway down to my beloved writing studio; again, wrapped around by my beloved books, a large fireplace, antique desks, and the stark, modern-day technical necessities. And, as in the morning, God and my black Labradors join me. I have learned that the morning and the evening are God's favored times of our meeting. Yet I resist—not in huge, blatant ways, but by a few insidious habits.

I suppose this resistance to prayer is the bane most injurious to the keeping of the vows I have made to God. *Nonetheless*, I simply cannot shake loose of Paul's words to the Thessalonians: "Pray continually. Give thanks in every situation because this is God's will for you in Christ Jesus. Don't suppress the Spirit" (1 Thessalonians 5:17-19).

Too often our inclinations toward disciplined prayer come to nothing. It is here that we must wage our soul's warfare: the petty temptations of our youth are past; now we face a truly insidious enemy, which is the temptation to pray "tomorrow."

Of such thinking, C. S. Lewis told a story, included in the collection *Fern-Seed and Elephants and Other Essays.* Preparing for a trip to London, Lewis thought it a good idea to have his hair cut. Before he left his home, he learned that the reason for the London visit had been cancelled. Therefore, he decided to put off the haircut as well. However, a thought kept nagging at him to get a haircut anyway. Finally, wearied by that irksome thought, he decided to go ahead and get his hair cut. His barber

Scripture

"When you pray, don't be like hypocrites. They love to pray standing in the synagogues and on the street corners so that people will see them. I assure you, that's the only reward they'll get. But when you pray, go to your room, shut the door, and pray to your Father who is present in that secret place. Your Father who sees what you do in secret will reward you."

Matthew 6:5-6

was a Christian whom Lewis and his brother, Warren, counseled from time to time. The barber welcomed him, telling Lewis that he was praying that Lewis might stop in that day. Lewis realized that coming that very day, and no later, met the barber's desire for a conversation and advice from him.

All of this taken into account still leaves us with the question, How does one pray unceasingly? This leads us to the Jesus Prayer: "Lord Jesus Christ, Son of God, have mercy on me, a sinner." This prayer is described best in the contemplative classic *The Way of a Pilgrim*, attributed to an anonymous Russian peasant. It tells of a desert pilgrim who wanted to learn how to pray constantly, in keeping with the apostle Paul's admonition. Having tried many complicated prayer forms, to no avail, he finally sought the help of one of the Desert Fathers. All of the Desert Fathers and Mothers claimed that this ten-word prayer sums up the entire gospel. Every day countless Christians carry the Jesus Prayer within them; wherever they go, their hearts, minds, souls, and mouths are filled with this prayer.

The lesson of prayer is easy to learn, but putting prayer into one's daily routine must be made a habit or our life of prayer will be constantly frustrated. God has infinite time for us. Can we not spare some time for God?

5

The Trinity

Spiritual Reading

You may ask, "If we cannot imagine a three-personal Being, what is the good of talking about Him?" Well, there isn't any good talking about Him. The thing that matters is being actually drawn into that three-personal life, and that may begin any time.

Mere Christianity

On the Trinity
Rueben Job

Of all the Christian doctrines, the Trinity is perhaps the most difficult to comprehend. Poets and theologians have attempted to shed light upon the three-in-one nature of God by employing such suggestive terms as *light*, *fire*, *wind*, *dove*, *intercessor*, *comforter*, *paraclete*, and *advocate*. On the one hand, no one of these seems sufficient to fully describe the tripartite nature of the Godhead, whereas on the other hand, any perception of God apart from the other persons of the Trinity diminishes God's robust nature.

C. S. Lewis was a master at clarifying complex theological issues. He uses simple illustrations to explain the profound meaning of the concept of a trinitarian God. He draws on personal, everyday experience to illustrate the meaning of this complex theological issue. His efforts parallel those of the early church, for they, too, sought to explain what they were experiencing. Their theology, as ours, grew out of their experience. And they clearly experienced God in three distinct expressions.

Perhaps nowhere in Lewis's writings do we gain greater insight into his skills and ability to employ logic and theology to the tenants of the Christian doctrine than that which we find in his discussions of the Trinity. Lewis once responded to a woman who had written to him about her struggles with the concept that God is three persons in one. In his response to her query Lewis writes, "The doctrine that Our Lord was God *and* man does not mean that He was a human body which had God instead of the normal human soul. It means that a real man (human body *and* human soul) was in Him so united with the second person of the Trinity as to make one Person; just as in you and me a complete anthropoid animal" (*Letters of C. S. Lewis*).

In these few words Lewis quite convinces us that any attempt to define God as a one-dimensional being will always fall short of the robust character of God. Indeed, any attempt to portray God as less than a multipartite being is inadequate to describe the nature of the Godhead.

Perhaps the most mysterious of the three persons of the Trinity is the Holy Spirit. Certainly, the Holy Spirit is the least understood and, we might add, the most difficult to comprehend. As if to help us over this hump, Lewis writes, "We must remind ourselves that Christian theology does not believe God to be a person. It believes Him to be such that in Him a trinity of persons is consistent with a unity of Deity. In that sense it believes Him to be something very different from a person, just as a cube

Scripture

This is what God planned for the climax of all times: to bring all things together in Christ, the things in heaven along with the things on earth. We have also received an inheritance in Christ. We were destined by the plan of God, who accomplishes everything according to his design. We are called to be an honor to God's glory because we were the first to hope in Christ. You too heard the word of truth in Christ, which is the good news of your salvation. You were sealed with the promised Holy Spirit because you believed in Christ. The Holy Spirit is the down payment on our inheritance, which is applied toward our redemption as God's own people, resulting in the honor of God's glory.

Ephesians 1:10-14

in which six squares are consistent with the unity of the body is different from a square. (Flatlanders, attempting to imagine a cube, would either imagine the six squares coinciding, and thus destroy their distinctness, or else imagine them set out side by side, and thus destroy the unity. Our difficulties about the Trinity are of much the same kind)" (*Christian Reflections*).

We see that the Trinity has to do with the nature of God as a tripartite being, often termed the Godhead. Theologians have long attempted to define the three-in-one nature of God by emphasizing the minuteness and the expansiveness of God's character: God is small enough to set up housekeeping in the human heart while being expansive enough to inhabit the universe.

Now we begin to understand that God the invisible God set about to create and rule over what God created. God the visible God, the second person of the Trinity, draped God's self within a cloak of human flesh and came teaching and healing. The ineffable God (the third person of the Trinity) draped God's self over the utter vastness of God's temporal and eternal creations, making God everywhere present to all people, at all times, in every nation, all of the time! This God is everywhere present, invited or rejected, recognized or ignored.

Thus God is made known to us in three manifestations that are always beyond our capacity to fully comprehend, yet always available to become more known in trusting, loving, and faithful relationship.

6

Worship

Spiritual Reading

No Christian and, indeed, no historian should accept the epigram which defines religion as "what a man does with his solitude." It was one of the Wesleys, I think, who said that the New Testament knows nothing of solitary religion. We are forbidden to neglect the assembling of ourselves together. Christianity is already institutional in the earliest of its documents. The Church is the Bride of Christ. We are members of one another.

The Weight of Glory and
Other Addresses

On Worship

Perry Bramlett

Exactly what is worship? It derives from the Old English word *worthship*, and various time-honored definitions of the outward expression of worship include "to honor or revere as holy," "to adore with appropriate acts, rites and ceremonies," and "to regard with extreme respect and devotion." What distinguishes the worship of God from our personal relationships is an all-pervading recognition of the absolute *worth* of God, for he alone is God, and our mind and heart, as the Psalmist wrote, cannot think of or desire anything greater. We must understand that authentic worship is not a game or "mere" ritual and that *always* we must be prepared to encounter the awesomeness and power of God. There are many more definitions of and ideas about worship, but most would agree today that in authentic worship we honor God, we praise God, we adore God, we communicate with God, we obey God . . . and sometimes, we encounter him.

We need worship. It is the best reason to go to church. When we worship in a church setting, we can know that if we really want to find God, we will find him. But if we come out of habit, or just because "it's Sunday," we are missing the point. If we come to church to be entertained, or "because of the pastor," or for the music, or just for social reasons, or for what the church "can do for the kids," we are missing the point. These are all well and good, but they are not the primary reason for worship. If we can come to an understanding of authentic worship, we can know that worship will refresh and renew us.

One of the interesting aspects about C. S. Lewis's life is that he almost did not become a Christian *because* of what he encountered in worship services. As a boy, he and his family attended worship regularly at their church in Belfast. Unfortunately, the pastor (his grandfather) preached sermons, though often elegant and verbally impressive, tainted by his intense prejudices toward Roman Catholics, whom he considered "the Devil's own children." This "loveless and graceless" preaching (often accompanied with crying spells) alienated Lewis, and probably was a factor (along with several others) that contributed to his early atheism.

And for much of his life he also disliked hymns sung at church and most other church music. He detested the "compulsory hymn singing" that soldiers had to endure (Lewis fought in and was wounded in World War I). He considered the lyrics of many hymns to be bad poetry;

Scripture

*Sing to the L*ORD*, all the earth!*
Share the news of his saving work every single day!
Declare God's glory among the nations;
declare his wondrous works among all people
*because the L*ORD *is great and so worthy of praise.*
He is awesome beyond all other gods
because all the gods of the nations are just idols,
*but it is the L*ORD *who created heaven!*
Greatness and grandeur are in front of him;
strength and joy are in his place.
*Give to the L*ORD*, all families of the nations—*
*give to the L*ORD *glory and power!*
*Give to the L*ORD *the glory due his name!*
Bring gifts! Enter his presence!
*Bow down to the L*ORD
in his holy splendor!

1 Chronicles 16:23-29

they were often too sentimental and "cheap" for his tastes and frequently contained what he believed to be "erroneous thought." The hymns he heard "shouted" at worship services were not good singing and were not, as he said, "the offering of our natural gifts at their highest to God." Lewis maintained that he preferred fewer, better, and shorter hymns in worship—"especially fewer."

As Lewis matured in his Christian faith, he came to realize that one's *attitude* toward worship and church music was what was important to God. He knew that God looked on the attitude and intention of a person's heart. If a hymn was sung or played, even badly, with an attitude of love and service, then it was favored by God. He compared this to the "intrinsically worthless" present from a child to its father; what the father values most is the loving *intention* of the gift. Lewis also learned that differing tastes in music and hymns could lead to a lesson in exercising spiritual humility and love, as he observed when he saw a "charwoman in the next pew" who loved all hymns and was probably a better Christian than he was. Good taste in music, he declared, "was not necessary to salvation."

Another problem for Lewis, as it is for many today, was that he disliked the "busyness" of so many worship services, with all the talk and loudness and irreverence. He favored private prayer and meditation and, if he was traveling, always chose a small, quiet church in which to worship. But while at home in Oxford he attended several services at his church each week and also worshipped at his college chapel.

An important lesson we can learn from Lewis concerning worship has to do with tradition. He believed it was necessary to attend worship services regularly because he knew that the regular gathering, throughout the history of the church, of the community of saints was traditional. And although at times he did not enjoy all worship services, he believed that it was his duty to attend and participate. This sustained commitment became a source of spiritual nourishment for Lewis, and he discovered that over the years, he became profoundly grateful for the experience of worship.

Someone has said that when we worship God with integrity, we "step back" from our routines and think about God: who he is, what he has done for us, how his love sustains us and our world, and his purpose for us as we live in his world. We should not worship because we think we are obligated, or because we think that God keeps a heavenly checklist with our name on it, or because we think we are doing God a favor. We worship because of who God is and because we must. Worship provides us spiritual renewal and refreshment. We would wither up and die spiritually if we did not stay close to our life source.

Either our existence is organized and centered around ourselves, or it is organized and centered around our Creator. We are, as a preacher once said, "either possessed

by God or possessed by ourselves." With our busy sched-
ules, we sometimes forget about God and what he has
done and is doing for us; our God does not care how we
sing, or what we wear, or where we sit, or what office we
hold. Are we giving ourselves to such a loving God, or are
we keeping to ourselves?

7

God

Spiritual Reading

God is basic Fact or Actuality, the
source of all other facthood. At
all costs therefore He must not be
thought of as a featureless generality.
If He exists at all, He is the most
concrete thing there is, the most
individual, "organized and minutely
articulated." He is unspeakable not
by being indefinite but by being too
definite for the unavoidable vagueness
of language.

Miracles

On God

Norman Shawchuck

Many of us never take the necessary pains to take a long loving look at God. Many of us wax eloquent about God and God's attributes without ever having taken a careful, thoughtful look at who God is according to God's own claims. C. S. Lewis took God seriously and sought to understand as much as he could about the nature, character, and activity of God.

Who *is* God? Such questions have occupied the thinking of humanity from the time of the seminal event in the garden of Eden, when Adam and Eve decided it was too risky to be close to God and decided to hide from God. From that time forward humanity has been asking two questions: Who is God? and Who is God for me?

We must not become so caught up in seeking answers to these questions so as to forget that God also comes querying, "Who am I—for you?" We must take this question most seriously. God does! When God in Christ asked the disciples, "Who do people say that I am? . . .

And what about you? Who do you say that I am?" (Mark 8:27, 29), God was asking a cosmic question directed to each and all who bear the burden of humanity; and therefore, we, too, must reply. The response we offer will for us make all the difference in how we view and live in this world and in the world to come.

In the times of the psalmist and the prophets the question, Who is God? occupied much of human thinking. To the woman at the well (John 4:24-26), Jesus explained: "'God is spirit, and it is necessary to worship God in spirit and truth.' The woman said, 'I know that the Messiah is coming, the one who is called the Christ. When he comes, he will teach everything to us.' Jesus said to her, 'I Am—the one who speaks with you.'"

Equally astounding is the exchange between Saul and Jesus: "Saul asked, 'Who are you, Lord?' 'I am Jesus, whom you are harassing,' came the reply" (Acts 9:5). And so it was that Saul, the belligerent enemy of God, came face to face (though he did not know it) with the Living Answer to his cosmic question. Saul's question is cosmic because it is the question of all humanity—and, we may assume that Lewis would say, "of all living creatures." God is all of this and more.

And so we have the invisible God and the visible God, and encompassing all of this is the Holy Spirit, the third person of the Trinity, the third person of God. We might assume that God arranged this in order that we might come to God without being burned, destroyed,

Scripture

Moses said to God, "If I now come to the Israelites and say to them, 'The God of your ancestors has sent me to you,' they are going to ask me, 'What's this God's name?'" . . . God said to Moses, "I Am Who I Am. . . . Say to the Israelites, 'The LORD, the God of your ancestors, Abraham's God, Isaac's God, and Jacob's God, has sent me to you.' This is my name forever; this is how all generations will remember me."

Exodus 3:13-15

or annihilated. As God told Moses, "No one can see me and live" (Exodus 33:20). And we observe in the written Word that the first business of God (the first person of the Trinity) was to create and rule over, while the business of Jesus (the second person of the Trinity) was to make God understandable to humans and to sustain, comfort, and save us from ourselves. God's nature is multifaceted: the triune Godhead is formed as a complex of three interrelated beings, which tradition identifies as Father, Son, and Holy Spirit (or Holy Ghost). Theologians attempt to shed light on this complexity by pointing out the minuteness and the expansiveness of God. What they are attempting to say to us is that God is both small enough to live in the human heart and expansive enough to permeate the universe.

As the psalmist tells us, there is nowhere we can go to hide from God (139:7-12). The overarching design of God, it seems, is to bring us humans to our true home in God. God's plan for this is made most explicit in the flesh-and-blood story of Jesus, the Son of God, who was born of God and who is God-in-the-flesh.

The author of Hebrews says, "In the past, God spoke through the prophets to our ancestors in many times and many ways. In these final days, though, he spoke to us through a Son. God made his Son the heir of everything and created the world through him" (1:1-2). Lewis found, as do we, the best picture of the nature and character of God in the birth, life, death, and resurrection of Jesus.

I think Lewis would say that we often look *at* the stories and accounts of Jesus in the Gospels rather than look *along* them. When we look along an event or assertion, we see a very different picture than when we simply look at the same event or assertion.

It is more desirable for us, especially we who are theologians, teachers, and pastors who handle and interpret the Scriptures to others, to look *along* the biblical accounts of Jesus and his followers. Simply to look *at* Jesus's words and actions and then to cast our votes regarding their authenticity is not enough. The more reflective and expansive seeing will surely increase our understanding of God and our relationship to God.

8

Evil

Spiritual Reading

There is no neutral ground in the universe: every square inch, every split second, is claimed by God and counterclaimed by Satan.

Christian Reflections

On Evil

Rueben Job

Evil appears to have had an early start with humankind. Genesis 2:4b-17 presents a picture of the beautiful garden of Eden that is already home to the tree of knowledge of good and evil. Adam and Eve began their life together in the presence of good and evil. While the Genesis text is debated, there is little argument about the reality of good and evil in the creation story or in the history of humankind that follows.

We could be led to think that Adam and Eve were given unfair treatment in their sudden exposure to evil. However, we may want to remember that upon the baptism and affirmation that he was God's beloved son, Jesus was immediately driven into the wilderness. There he experienced forty days of wrestling with evil in its most inviting and destructive mask. Jesus was tempted to believe that good can be achieved by evil means. Evil seems to have been on the stage from the very beginning and thoughtful people have wrestled with the concept ever since.

C. S. Lewis was among those who puzzled over the existence of evil. So much of his writing deals with this question. He sees it as a theological problem that pushes us to examine the very nature of God. Can we accept a dualism that pits good and evil against each other? If we do, we must push beyond good and evil to the ultimate Creator. The most rational response to the problem of good and evil is found in monotheism. But questions remain, and throughout his writing Lewis addresses this issue again and again. It is a problem that has perplexed thoughtful persons in every generation, including our own.

With terrorism becoming a powerful political strategy and more common practice, the world is forced to stare at the face of evil as much as it had to confront it during two world wars and the cold war. Rocket attacks, suicide bombers, and mass shootings are now a threat to everyone and every place. The slaughter of innocents by the thousands, child warriors, and the starvation of children put a human face on the horrible and devastating consequences of evil.

Today we see pictures of suffering that are as haunting as those of the concentration camps and ghettoes of the first half of the twentieth century. Evil was not difficult to find in Lewis's time, and it is easily found in our world. Where is evil at its worst? What is its origin? Lewis struggles with these questions and offers no easy and simple answers.

Identifying that which is evil seems easy, but finding

Scripture

You were once darkness, but now you are light in the Lord, so live your life as children of light. Light produces fruit that consists of every sort of goodness, justice, and truth. Therefore, test everything to see what's pleasing to the Lord, and don't participate in the unfruitful actions of darkness. Instead, you should reveal the truth about them. It's embarrassing to even talk about what certain persons do in secret. But everything exposed to the light is revealed by the light. Everything that is revealed by the light is light. Therefore, it says, Wake up, sleeper! Get up from the dead, and Christ will shine on you.

Ephesians 5:8-14

some rational explanation for evil's existence is almost as difficult as it is to root it out, expose it to the light of truth, and hasten its demise. Lewis remains convinced that evil was a secondary force in the world and not a first cause. He believes that God was always above and beyond evil and also able to use evil for good.

Suffering is not a good, but Lewis believes it could lead to a good. It could lead people to seek God's will, develop greater compassion, and pursue more acts of mercy. In these ways, he says in *The Problem of Pain,* God salvages some good from evil.

Sometimes evil and good lie as choices before us, as the tree of the knowledge of good and evil did for Adam and Eve. These choices are often difficult and hidden among much that is good and desirable. Challenging as it is, often we can see the costly consequences of making wrong choices in our own lives. However, even the wrong choices can teach us the better way.

The more difficult to explain and endure are those unannounced and unprovoked torrents of evil that pummel the innocent and the just. Why does suffering visit the innocent? Why does a terminal disease take a young father from his family, a woman at the peak of her career, a beautiful and promising child from a loving family? Until we have wrestled with such questions, we are avoiding or glossing over the grim reality of pain and evil that is so evident in the world. This is where Lewis bravely leads the reader as he confesses his own struggle with his wife's terminal illness. He and Helen Joy Davidman met as intellectual explorers, became platonic friends, and eventually allowed their relationship to blossom into a deep and abiding love. They married when she was already fighting a disease that eventually took her life. There were times of great ecstasy and joy in their brief marriage, and upon his wife's death, Lewis faced the darkness as never before.

He had become one of the world's most articulate defenders of the Christian faith, but in the depths of his grief he began to wonder if his view of God had been too simple and complimentary. When you are happy, it is easier to approach God with gratitude, he noted in *A Grief Observed*. But when you seek God in desperation, it can feel like a door has slammed in your face. What Lewis discovered in the courage to face cancer, death, and a palpable aloneness, without blinking or turning away, was a path that led him from doubt to affirmation of the reality, wisdom, and goodness of God.

Lewis's pain, fear, anxiety, grief, and loss never diminished, yet he never allowed them to conquer faith or life. He wrestled with the deep theological problems of evil as a brilliant intellectual, and he confronted the reality of pain, the evils of war, and ravages of disease as a loving, finite mortal. The wisdom he gleans and shares continues to bless those who follow a path that seeks intellectual honesty and uncompromising faith in a God of unqualified love.

9

The Bible

Spiritual Reading

The human qualities of the raw
materials show through. Naivety, error,
contradiction, even (as in the cursing
Psalms) wickedness are not removed.
The total result is not "the Word of
God" in the sense that every passage,
in itself, gives impeccable science or
history. It carries the Word of God;
and we (under grace, with attention to
tradition and to interpreters wiser than
ourselves, and with the use of such
intelligence and learning as we may
have) receive that word from it not
by using it as an encyclopedia or an
encyclical but by steeping ourselves in
its tone or temper and so learning its
overall message.

Letters of C. S. Lewis

On the Bible

Perry Bramlett

It is interesting, and just a little curious, that there has been comparatively little written about C. S. Lewis and the Bible. In a careful study of his letters, books, and essays, one will find that Lewis had a balanced approach to the Scriptures, and this is reflected in what he wrote. He wrote about the Bible as literature; individual books of the Bible (particularly the Psalms); biblical inspiration and revelation; biblical translations; how the Bible should be approached, read, and studied; biblical scholarship; and more. Furthermore, thanks to his own accounts and the testimonies of family and friends, we know that Lewis loved Holy Scripture; read and studied them as often as his health allowed; and considered the Bible to be the holy, inspired Word of God, with Jesus Christ as its center and the starting point for all study and devotion.

Lewis, however, did not worship the Bible. He did not believe that God's revealed, written word was the *only* way to truth, and after years of study and thought, he came to believe that God used other methods alongside the Bible to show Godself and God's Son. Some of these other revelations include literature, certain parts of other religions and faiths, some myths and stories, reason, nature, art, and music. All of these, Lewis claimed, had the stamp of God's inspiration on them, and the thoughtful Christian ignored them at his or her peril.

Some Christians today confess confusion over the choosing of a Bible translation. There are so many of these, plus paraphrases, study Bibles, and specialty Bibles (which seem to be published almost daily), that choosing the "right" Bible translation can be a problem, particularly for the young and inexperienced Christian. Lewis emphasized that a Bible reader should *understand* the Bible, and thus Lewis was open to reading and studying modern translations, and he recommended their use. Perhaps his favorite version was James Moffatt's New Translation, which he judged to be particularly good. He showed his ecumenical spirit by endorsing Fr. Ronald Knox's Catholic translation of the New Testament. Lewis never mentioned reading or studying The Jerusalem Bible, for which his great friend J. R. R. Tolkien translated the Book of Jonah. Lewis would regularly read from the Authorized Version (also known as the King James Version), and also from J. B. Phillips's translation of the New Testament, for which he wrote an introduction for the first volume of this translation, called "*Letters to Young Churches.*" In his introduction to Phillips, Lewis revealed that he enjoyed learning new truth and was not bound

Scripture

The LORD's Instruction is perfect,
reviving one's very being.
The LORD's laws are faithful,
making naive people wise.
The LORD's regulations are right,
gladdening the heart.
The LORD's commands are pure,
giving light to the eyes.
Honoring the LORD is correct,
lasting forever.
The LORD's judgments are true.
All of these are righteous!
They are more desirable than gold—
than tons of pure gold!
They are sweeter than honey—
even dripping off the honeycomb!
No doubt about it:
your servant is enlightened by them;
there is great reward in keeping them.

Psalm 19:7-11

by tradition, writing that the Authorized Version was no longer a clear translation and its English was outdated and used words that now have different meanings. We must continue to develop new translations of the Bible, he said, because if we don't have new ones, people will be less likely to read the Bible.

Lewis read the Bible for several reasons. First, for its literary beauty, solemnity, and its awesome antiquity, for its *feel* of history and of the ancient. A word he sometimes used, *quiddity*, illuminates this view, as it means the essential nature of a thing. Second, he read the Scriptures devotionally to try to start to understand the great doctrines and themes of faith and to gain an idea of the whys and wherefores of the church and Christian community.

It is important to note that Lewis *read* and *studied* the Bible. An author has written that in good Bible study, the student masters the text, while in good Bible reading, the Bible masters the student. Lewis is a model for us in that he did both. In so doing, he took seriously and followed faithfully the words from the Book of Common Prayer, which affirms that God's intention for Holy Scripture is that we should "inwardly digest them" so that we might "ever hold fast" to the salvation we receive by Jesus Christ.

Lewis's comments on the Bible commend us to study it to try to understand it, in whatever version we find most accessible. Further, his example teaches us to read the Bible with an open mind and spirit, allowing ourselves to be transformed by it.

10

Devotional Life

Spiritual Reading

It is Christ Himself, not the Bible, who is the true word of God. The Bible, read in the right spirit and with the guidance of good teachers, will bring us to Him. . . . But we must not use the Bible (our fathers too often did) as a sort of Encyclopedia out of which texts (isolated from their contexts and not read with attention to the whole nature and purport of the books in which they occur) can be taken for use as weapons.

Reflections on the Psalms

On Devotional Life

Perry Bramlett

Lewis strongly believed in an active devotional life, with the Bible at its center. He read the Scriptures virtually every day and combined his reading with prayer. His mother, Flora, taught him the value of the Book of Common Prayer, and from his early exposure to this Anglican liturgical work he learned, and deliberately maintained (after he became a Christian), a balanced approach to his reading of the Bible. For his daily devotional time he would read a passage from the Old Testament (often the Psalms) and one from the New Testament, usually the Gospels (particularly Mark's Gospel, believed to be the first written), and sometimes from Paul's writings. He enjoyed reading the New Testament in Greek, and we could surmise that he likely read the Old Testament in Hebrew. Lewis always went back to primary sources and loved reading from any older or ancient text or writing. In a letter to a correspondent he mentioned that he read from the Vulgate (a fourth-century Latin translation) and recommended especially the Book of Acts in this venerable translation.

The Bible was Lewis's primary vehicle to God. His gradual perception of its central message helped him come to a clear knowledge of his Creator, then to faith in Christ and a life of authentic discipleship. His chief reason for reading the Bible was to find Jesus, whom he called the "sacred fish." Lewis came to understand that the Bible ultimately reveals Jesus and that our Lord's teaching ("that darting illumination") could be incorporated into his life only when he sought Jesus with his whole heart and mind. Thus, he read the Gospel accounts of Jesus not as biographies but as God's Word, through Jesus, to him. Someone has written that reading the Bible is both praying and listening, and that is how Lewis read, with an "attitude of prayer" and a willingness to listen for whatever God might be saying to him, personally, in the hallowed pages of Scripture.

The Bible was for him the best guide (combined with prayer) to authentic Christian living, and Lewis immersed himself in its overall message. In particular, he gleaned from the pages of the Scriptures (and from his Christian friends) the best examples of how Christians are to treat their neighbors, starting with Jesus's love and acceptance for all people. And Lewis learned about heaven from his devotional reading of the Bible. He said he wrote about heaven in nearly all of his books, and for him, the beautiful biblical pictures of heaven, though symbolic, were

Scripture

The Word became flesh
*   and made his home among us.*
We have seen his glory,
*   glory like that of a father's only son,*
*   full of grace and truth.*

John 1:14

"bright blurs" that stayed with him his entire Christian life.

Lewis's devotional practice is a wonderful example for today's Christians. He believed that the Bible, when received in faith and in the right spirit, would lead its reader to salvation and to the right path(s) of victorious Christian discipleship. He encouraged his readers (particularly in *Reflections on the Psalms*) to look for the overall message of the Bible ("steeping ourselves in its tone or temper") and not to employ it to try to win theological arguments or doctrinal battles. He also urged using it faithfully in the worship of God in the church. For Lewis, the Bible was "God's vehicle of truth" that carried God's Word to the reader, who, when approaching the Scriptures with a prayerful and receptive attitude, would become perhaps a little "inspired" as well.

11

Sin

Spiritual Reading

It is natural to feel that if *all men* are as
bad as the Christians say, then badness
must be very excusable. If all the boys
[fail] the examination, surely the
papers must have been too hard?

The Problem of Pain

On Sin

Rueben Job

Every parent has heard a child say, "But every other parent lets their daughter/son go" to the party, the movie, or you fill in the blank. As frequently as the argument is used, usually it will not win release from parental oversight or childhood accountability. C. S. Lewis knows how quick we are to say, "Well, everyone does it."

What would it hurt if I fudge just a little on my taxes, take a pencil home from work, or nibble on a grape or strawberry as I pick up the rest of my groceries? Everyone else does! But it does not end there. The nibbled grape dulls the sense of right and wrong, the pencil taken clouds the lines of ownership and integrity, and all begin to blur the lines between good and bad, right and wrong. Sin is insidious and if allowed entrance and left unattended, it will ultimately invade and take control of all of life in ever more destructive and harmful ways.

It is true that sometimes we take sin too lightly and dismiss all sin as insignificant. After all, we believe ourselves to be in control and we bow to no one. From this vantage point I can do what I want, when I want, and no harm or consequence will arise that I cannot handle. And this of course is the root of all sin and the greatest sin of all: our replacing God with ourselves. The more we move in the direction of placing ourselves at the center of all things, the deeper we move into a life dominated by that which is contrary to and not in harmony with God and God's will.

Taking sin too lightly is to put ourselves and our relationship with God and others at risk. The opposite extreme is equally dangerous and destructive. Often, we take sin too seriously; we give it too much power in and over our lives. From this vantage point we see ourselves as helpless victims, all too prone to sin and helpless to overcome the hold sin has upon our lives. This can lead to self-hatred and despair, which cripples and crushes all that is good and joyful out of the gift of life. Lewis had a much more balanced view of sin. He was fully aware of its insidious and dangerous nature and its devastating consequences. He was also deeply conscious of the promised remedy for sin.

Lewis recognized that it is often difficult for us to sense our own sin. We make excuses and are oblivious of our actions upon others because we concentrate so fully on ourselves and our needs. It is difficult for us to realize that our sin will be our ruin. Even the unrecognized sin left to roam freely within can destroy everything we value.

Scripture

So what are we going to say? Should we continue sinning so grace will multiply? Absolutely not! All of us died to sin. How can we still live in it? Or don't you know that all who were baptized into Christ Jesus were baptized into his death? Therefore, we were buried together with him through baptism into his death, so that just as Christ was raised from the dead through the glory of the Father, we too can walk in newness of life.

Romans 6:1-4

In *God in the Dock,* Lewis says it is easier to see this is true in others than it is to see it in ourselves.

All sins are deadly but not all sins are equal. Lewis believed that the basic sin behind all sin was to put ourselves rather than God at the center of all things. Once we have placed ourselves there, everything we do we will decide on the basis of what is best for us and not on the basis of truth, right, wrong, the needs of others, or the will and desire of God. Once we have replaced God with ourselves, we no longer have a standard against which to measure and no doorkeeper to our soul. And then every other sin will have easy access to our lives.

Lewis distinguishes between the levels of "badness" of sin. "Sins of the flesh" are often more highly criticized but are not the worst of all sins. The spiritual sins of pride, power, hatred, and spite are much more destructive, he says in *Mere Christianity.* Our church culture seems quick to spot and criticize the sins of the flesh but slow to identify and seek remedy for the sins of the spirit. The sins involving sex are dramatized and sensationalized, and we scold and fuss over them. And yet, we are unmoved by greed, avarice, and acquisitiveness, which result in great disparity between rich and poor and leave thousands starving in a world of plenty.

Fortunately, this is not the end of the story. Sin is destructive and deadly, but it is not all-powerful. God is all-powerful, and therein is our hope. The remedy of sin is found in confession, repentance, and steadfast faith in our

Savior, Jesus Christ. God loves us just as we are and not as we were or will become. God alone has the power to cleanse and declare us forgiven. God always seeks to call us forth into being more than we are as God forgives and invites us to live whole and holy lives.

Sin confessed, repented, and forgiven is forever gone. Of course, the scars may remain for a lifetime, but the sin and the consequences of a broken relationship with God are cancelled forever. Forgiven sin has no power within or over us. God's act of forgiveness restores a right relationship, and once more nothing stands between us and God. We recognize ourselves as sinners forgiven and guilt free with a clean page upon which to write the story of our lives.

Amazing as it seems, not only are we called to obedient and faithful living but also we are offered strength and companionship to fulfill our calling. As Scripture tells us, all have sinned and fallen short of the glory of God and all are offered the gift of redemption in Christ Jesus (Romans 3:23-24 and Matthew 26:28). This redemption is complete and results in a joyful discipleship. Sin can be a powerful force in our lives, but God is more powerful and completely willing and able to set us free from sin and its trailing load of guilt.

12

Christian Marriage

Spiritual Reading

The modern tradition is that the proper reason for marrying is the state described as "being in love." Now I have nothing to say against "being in love": but the idea that this is or ought to be the exclusive reason or that it can ever be by itself an *adequate* basis seems to me simply moonshine.

Letters of C. S. Lewis

On Christian Marriage

Norman Shawchuck

C. S. Lewis was a bachelor for most of life until a woman from America wandered into his life. Her name was Helen Joy Davidman. Joy had recently divorced her husband, and deciding to put distance between them, she went to England. Soon after arriving in London, Joy met Lewis. Eventually they were married and for a while enjoyed sheer bliss. Lewis entered into a wonderful and altogether too brief phase of his life, filled with new learning about the spiritual and human dynamics of marriage. Joy's life was soon to be taken by cancer. Lewis was thrust into deep pain and sorrow, out of which flowed some of his most prolific writing as he attempted to describe the ecstasy and pain of his brief days with Joy. Of his marriage and sorrow Lewis wrote:

> "It was too perfect to last," so I am tempted to say of our marriage. . . . But it could also mean "This had reached its proper perfection. This had become

what it had in it to be. Therefore of course it would
not be prolonged." As if God said, "Good; you have
mastered that exercise. I am very pleased with it.
And now you are ready to go on to the next." (*A
Grief Observed*)

Soon after Joy's death, Sheldon Vanauken, a young
man from America, enrolled in studies under Lewis
at Oxford University, where Lewis was serving as
Oxford's most noted professor and as a lecturer. Lewis
and Vanauken soon became dear friends. Interestingly,
Vanauken would walk the same pathway of grief as did
Lewis before him. Sheldon's young wife, Davy, died of
cancer on July 13, 1960. Out of this sorrow flowed some
of the most poignant writing about joy, pain, death,
sorrow, and loss, as Vanauken labored to record his life
with Davy and his abject grief.

One can hardly think of Lewis's works without also
looking into the writings of Sheldon Vanauken, without
doubt one of Lewis's most beloved students at Oxford.
Their experiences of life, love, and marriage parallel in
a most poignant manner. Vanauken, like Lewis, would
become a noted writer as he labored to record his sorrow.
Vanauken wrote two soulful books brimming with the
savor of Lewis's writing: *A Severe Mercy* and *Gateway to
Heaven*.

As Lewis before him, Vanauken converted to the
Christian faith. Each of the men suffered the death of
their spouses, but while their spouses lived the couples

Scripture

Love should be shown without pretending. . . . Be the best at showing honor to each other.

Romans 12:9-10

experienced "fairy-tale like" love and joy mingled with the bittersweet.

Like Sheldon and Davy, Jack and Joy were devoted to each other. Yet, around their marriage flurried many rumors and much controversy. Nonetheless, a careful reading of the information at our disposal leads us to believe that Lewis and Joy were deeply in love, and Joy's death dealt Lewis a most serious blow from which he never fully recovered. Sometime later Lewis mused on whether those who have died also grieve separation from their beloved; could this be an experience of purgatory? he wondered. Mourning is part of the experience of love, he said.

Many couples presenting themselves for marriage may believe, or at least hope, that their marriage will be perfect. We may wish that every couple rehearses their marriage vows with good intentions. However, the statistics of marriage and divorce in the United States make it clear that, in marriage, good intentions are not enough to keep a marriage and family together.

Certainly Lewis's marriage to Joy was foundational to opening an entirely new vista of life. Marriage is basically a community of two in which both parties seek always to outdo the other in love and devotion. When this happens, marriage brings great meaning to the partners and unusual witness and strength to the larger community.

13

Jesus

Spiritual Reading

"What are we to make of Christ?"
There is no question of what we can
make of Him, it is entirely a question
of what He intends to make of us.

God in the Dock

On Jesus

Perry Bramlett

All of us take Jesus seriously, don't we? Most of the readers of this book would claim to, and they would probably have certain things in common. We attend the church Jesus founded (if it is a Christian church), we pray to him over meals and at special occasions, we believe (or say we believe) certain things about him, we think that his life was a good example, we believe that his teachings were good and noble and should be emulated (at least some of the time), and some of us even try to follow him and be, at least casually, his disciple. Many of us also sing hymns dedicated to him and take our children to a church that tells stories about him, and a lot of us (according to polls) believe that he was the greatest person in all of history. It would be an insult to many of us if someone were to suggest that we do not take Jesus seriously.

How can, and should, a person take Jesus seriously? William H. Willimon, a retired United Methodist bishop, wrote that one of the great heresies of American popular religion is the "me and Jesus" arrangement. People who practice this theology portray Jesus as a close personal friend; one who always listens, comforts, and agrees; and who almost never challenges or offends. In this privatized view, Jesus is not the ethically demanding Christ of the New Testament, but rather the one who figuratively pours oil and wine over our wounds, always helping us to feel better. It pays scarce attention to Jesus the Lord over the community of believers, the body of Christ, and our communal discipleship. The Jesus who preached the rigorous social and ethical demands of the Sermon on the Mount is relegated to a cozy Christ who is there when *we* need him. His command to love our neighbors as ourselves, his admonition to challenge the evil principalities and powers of the world, and his strong demands that we feed the poor, heal the sick, and witness to his kingdom are conveniently forgotten. Jesus is a friend all right, but the friend that we need, not necessarily want.

Lewis never wrote a book about Jesus, but it is very evident he took Jesus seriously. Sometimes Lewis seems almost to have gone out of his way to avoid mentioning Jesus in his books and letters. When he wrote or mentioned God the Son, Lewis often used "our Lord," sometimes "Christ," and once "the holiest of all petitioners." Lewis scholars have wondered about this, speculating that Lewis was not comfortable with Jesus and the whole idea of God's humanity. It's possible that Lewis, being a gentleman, was merely trying not to be overly

Scripture

Adopt the attitude that was in Christ Jesus:

> *Though he was in the form of God,*
> *he did not consider being equal with God some-*
> *thing to exploit.*
> *But he emptied himself*
> *by taking the form of a slave*
> *and by becoming like human beings.*

Philippians 2:5-7

familiar with Jesus. Likely he was being reverent, an attitude badly needed today.

Lewis held traditional views about Jesus, and his beliefs were largely shaped by the great historic creeds of Christianity. He saw Jesus as both human and divine, fully God and fully man, Lord and Savior. He accepted the virgin birth and other miracles and believed that the New Testament provided an accurate account of the life of Jesus. Lewis saw Jesus as the Son of God and often quoted the New Testament in affirming that the best and most accurate picture of God is the one we have in Jesus.

He did not care for atonement theories (probably because there were so many) and emphasized that although we cannot fully understand how the atonement (Jesus's sacrificial death) worked, we can accept in faith that Jesus's death somehow has given us a fresh start.

Lewis's witness to the world is that he did take Jesus seriously. What made Jesus unique for Lewis was the nature of Jesus's will. Jesus refused to submit to temptations and weaknesses, and despite the fact that he was human and had feelings, he gave us a perfect example of obedience and self-sacrifice. And in Jesus, Lewis saw a man who was all that we were intended to be. Jesus was the perfect person, the great model of life and living. Time after time in his writings Lewis presented this Jesus clearly and creatively, the man who was the Christ of the Bible.

14

Running from God

Spiritual Reading

It has been admitted throughout that
man has free will and that all gifts to
him are therefore two-edged. From
these premises it follows directly that
the Divine labour to redeem the world
cannot be certain of succeeding as
regards every individual soul. Some
will not be redeemed.

The Problem of Pain

On Running from God

Norman Shawchuck

Running from God is a race run in the heart, mind, and soul of the runners that is reflected in every facet of the runners' lives. For many years, C. S. Lewis was a runaway seeking escape from God. He was an avowed atheist until he became a Christian in 1931. Thereafter, he would invest his time and energies in writing, teaching, and public speaking, much in the manner of Jesus and the apostle Paul.

There are many avenues by which people may run from God. We may merely turn a deaf ear to God's Word offered to us by inner voice or by written, spoken, or lived testimony. We may choose not to feed or clothe our neighbors or heal their physical or emotional wounds; and by so doing, we distance ourselves from God and our neighbors.

Lewis is quite clear that while we may run from God, we can never evade God. God is everywhere, Lewis said, whether we can see God or not. When Jesus extends to us the invitation to "come to me, all you who are struggling hard and carrying heavy loads, and I will give you rest" (Matthew 11:28), and we ignore him, we are running from God. It is quite safe to assume that we all know this, yet running from God seems to be an inborn tendency of human nature.

If I am blind and deaf and someone calls to me from across the distance and I fail to move in the caller's direction, I am not intentionally moving away from the one who is calling. But if I have sight and hearing, and I hear the Voice that is calling and I turn a deaf ear, am I not running from the One who is calling me?

It does seem that sooner or later, we all seek to evade God's call and claims upon us. The prodigal (Luke 15:11-22) ran from his generous father and spent his inheritance only to end up with pigs in their poverty. And then he ran some more until he fell into the arms of his father, who seemed to be watching for him. We can imagine the father asking, "What took you so long?"

Did not the father's ever-obedient elder son also run from his father? Arguably, he had been running from his father for many years, even though he never left the confines of the farm fields. He ran from his father's love and largess; in his mind he was keeping score. At the end of the day he, too, returned to the father, churlish and very much unappreciative.

You and I are often that son! Even a cursory reading of the Scriptures is enough to convince us that running from God is a universal phenomenon.

Scripture

The LORD's word came to Jonah, Amittai's son: "Get up and go to Nineveh, that great city, and cry out against it, for their evil has come to my attention." So Jonah got up—to flee to Tarshish from the LORD!

Jonah 1:1-3

It seems that the people of God have long been running from God, perhaps not with their feet but in their hearts and minds. The prophet Isaiah tells us that the Lord said, "These people turn toward me with their mouths, and honor me with lip service while their heart is distant from me, and their fear of me is just a human command that has been memorized" (Isaiah 29:13).

In his famous poem "The Hound of Heaven," Francis Thompson, an earlier contemporary of Lewis (1859–1907), depicts the attempt to run from God as an exercise in futility. Lewis knew this poem well, and in it he would have seen much of his own journey from atheism to Christianity.

We can seek God or run from God. Job, Jonah, the writer of Psalm 139, Julian of Norwich, and Lewis share this. The happiness is in the seeking, the misery in the denial. We are prodigal sons and daughters of God, awaiting the wedding feast of lessons, stories, and parables given to us by the greatest of the great teachers, poets, and writers. Certainly, Lewis will have his place among these. Claiming their truth, we will be surprised to learn we no longer need to run from God.

15

Conversion

Spiritual Reading

Conversion requires an alteration of
the will, and an alteration which, in
the last resort, does not occur without
the intervention of the supernatural.

God in the Dock

On Conversion

Perry Bramlett

For many people, "salvation" describes something they believe they "have," "own," or has "happened" to them. They don't perceive that this has much to do with the actual living and doing of the Christian life. Either you have it or you don't, some say. Many believe also that salvation or conversion has a great deal to do with an emotional or initial "experience." A person responds to an altar call after a sermon and tells the preacher that he or she wants to be "saved." Or some may tell the pastor that they've had a private experience, have decided to become a Christian, and now desire to join the church.

Initial conversion experiences are not to be taken lightly. Often, an initial experience with God is the first step toward a long-lasting and fruitful Christian life. But for some people, that initial conversion experience, whether emotional or rational or both, is their only and *final* step. God's loving grace and free offer of salvation are seen not as powers that change but as insurance that grants an entrance to heaven and makes a person a Christian.

Contrary to this position, conversion is a *process*. It is not something we simply "have" and is not a one-time or past experience. A converted person is a soul under construction. As we respond to God in faith, God graciously and lovingly transforms us. Conversion is, as one theologian put it, a "gifted power" that changes us from what we are to what God intends us to be.

There was a man who "got religion" in the twilight of a notorious life. The change was so dramatic that he was always being asked to tell how he got saved. Eventually he wrote it out and stored the manuscript in his attic for safekeeping. One day the new preacher came to call and wanted to hear about the man's salvation experience. His wife went to the attic to get the paper. A little later she came bounding down the stairs and burst into the living room, her face white as a sheet. "Mice in the attic," she announced, "have chewed up your experience!" The problem with thinking of conversion or "being born again" as a past or one-time experience is that it has little to do with life *now*, and it has little to do with growth and commitment and discipleship. It has little to do with Jesus's urgent command to "follow me!"

C. S. Lewis's conversion to theism, or belief that a god exists, took about a dozen years or so, and he wrote about it in his autobiography, *Surprised by Joy*. His continued conversion took another two or three years.

Scripture

*Ananias . . . placed his hands on Saul and said,
"Brother Saul, the Lord sent me—Jesus, who appeared
to you on the way as you were coming here. He sent me
so that you could see again and be filled with the Holy
Spirit."*

Acts 9:17

Kathryn Lindskoog, a Lewis historian, said that Lewis came to believe that Christianity was true by using the tests of authority, reason, and experience. He accepted the authority of such Christians as G. K. Chesterton, George MacDonald, and others who taught and wrote about spiritual realities. His reasoned logic convinced him that belief in God and the fact of Jesus Christ made more sense than atheistic materialism. And he discovered in the lived experiences of colleagues such as J. R. R. Tolkien and others a quality of assurance and belief, which he lacked, in the supernatural. In addition, Lewis opened his mind and heart and made a conscious effort to examine and question the basic facts of Christian doctrine. What he found convinced him that his conversion would be a lifelong journey.

Lewis knew that intellect played a large part in his conversion. He also learned that emotions and feelings, while they have their good and proper place, should not be the fulcrum on which we base our conversion. He maintained that a person's conversion (and his own) should be built on a faith that continues to believe and trust what we know to be true, regardless of feelings.

The great example Lewis sets for us today is that he worked out his own conversion with fear and trembling, as it says in Philippians. After his initial decision to accept the truth of God and to follow Christ as a committed disciple, he set out to find the implications of his new faith. He examined the roots of sin in his life and reevaluated his personal relationships. He discovered that if his conversion was to continue, he must deal with his ambition and pride and turn over his life to the will of God. In a letter to a friend, he wrote that the real business of a Christian was not to succeed, but to *do right* and "leave the rest to God." That was his aim as a writer, a teacher, a member of a household, a husband, and a private citizen: to do right.

16

The Risk of Discipleship

Spiritual Reading

If conversion to Christianity makes
no improvement in a man's outward
actions—if he continues to be just
as snobbish or spiteful or envious or
ambitious as he was before—then
I think we must suspect that his
"conversion" was largely imaginary;
and after one's original conversion,
every time one thinks one has made an
advance, that is the test to apply. Fine
feelings, new insights, greater interest
in "religion" mean nothing unless they
make our actual behaviour better.

Mere Christianity

On the Risk
of Discipleship

Perry Bramlett

A pastor who grew up during World War II describes how, as a teenager, he once asked his church-school teacher if Hitler was a Christian. Her answer was one he never forgot. She said something like, "Well, he does not appear to be, but we can hope that when he was a little boy he gave his heart to Jesus. If he did, he is saved." Although he was young, he thought even then that Christianity must be weak. If a man who burns Jews and executes people every day is "saved" by one childhood experience, then his conversion must not have much to do with life.

The story is told of a man who once showed up at an old-fashioned revival meeting. He had a notorious, awful reputation. He was a convicted murderer, thief, and boot-legger, and was currently living with his fifth wife. During the very emotional service, he ran forward to testify to the audience. He said, speaking of his conversion, "I know when I got it, I know where I got it, and I know how to get it. I've treated it rough, but I've still got it." He then sat down to enthusiastic applause. We can presume that whatever "it" was, he indeed had "treated it rough."

These anecdotes show that many perceive conversion as having nothing whatsoever to do with the quality of one's life. Often the church, tacitly or explicitly, has encouraged this. But to take Jesus seriously also requires us to develop a passion for our own character. Whether we realize it or not, people are looking at us and watching us to see if our Christianity is genuine.

In a gospel hymn we sing "what a friend we have in Jesus," and it makes us feel good. It gently admonishes us to take our trials, temptations, and troubles to Jesus in prayer. However, the friend we have in Jesus is one who challenges us, examines us, calls us to authentic discipleship, and instructs us to look at the needs of others. This Jesus wants, perhaps more than anything else, for us to get out of ourselves. The teachings of Jesus and the New Testament are in direct opposition to a private relationship with God. To take Jesus seriously requires that we act on the fact that Christianity is an ethical, selfless, serving, following, loving, neighborly faith.

One important reason that conversion is called a gift is because it actually is a re-creation. It is not merely a changing of one's personality or disposition. A person who becomes truly converted is a new person. Sometimes the conversion event is labeled as being "born again,"

Scripture

Jesus said to everyone, "All who want to come after me must say no to themselves, take up their cross daily, and follow me. All who want to save their lives will lose them. But all who lose their lives because of me will save them. What advantage do people have if they gain the whole world for themselves yet perish or lose their lives?"

Luke 9:23-25

using the phrase from John 3:3. The words "born again" suggest the birthing process. Physical birth entails risk: the possibilities that the mother may die in childbirth or the infant will have physical or mental abnormalities or be lost through stillbirth. A mother knows the risks of giving birth. But in spiritual re-birth or conversion, the new Christian is not often told of the risks.

A man was considering Christian commitment and conversion. One of his friends asked him if he would consider turning his life over to Christ for one week, total. The man replied, "That's way too long." His friend: "How about one day?" The man: "Can't do it, too scary." His friend then asked, "How about one hour?" The man hesitated, then said, "Yes." The story goes that the man moved from taking the risk of conversion for one hour a week to a lifelong commitment.

As an old preacher once said, "The Christian who takes Jesus (and the world) seriously is the one who engages in a fighting struggle to get rid of sin and take on the character of Jesus." We are not only to struggle against those things we know and that others know are wrong but also to pray for new moral perception so that we will better understand what sin is according to the mind of Christ. And as the same old preacher said further, "Our new moral perception must start with love, and that love starts with us and spreads to our world."

17

Grief

Spiritual Reading

No one ever told me that grief felt so much like fear. I am not afraid, but the sensation is like being afraid. The same fluttering in the stomach, the same restlessness, the yawning.... At other times it feels like being mildly drunk, or concussed. There is a sort of invisible blanket between the world and me.

A Grief Observed

On Grief

Norman Shawchuck

Sooner or later grief comes to everyone; it is a part of the human condition. However, grief does not always invade the soul in the same manner. There is solitary grief, community grief, and national grief. The destruction of the twin towers of the World Trade Center, in New York City, on September 11, 2001, plunged Americans into deep canyons of profound sorrow. Few chose to be apart from the nation's collective grief. We pray and we hope that our national grief will serve to make us a better, more connected people.

No one completely evades grief. Even Jesus, the very Son of God, experienced and expressed abject grief. His agonized prayer in the garden of Gethsemane, as he emptied his anguished soul to God, is a cosmic example of this: "Now I am deeply troubled. What should I say? 'Father, save me from this time'? No, for this is the reason I have come to this time. Father, glorify your name!" (John 12:27-28).

We, too, can experience grief as consuming us with unimaginable pain, as though the gates of hell were opened to unleash their furies upon us. Such grief can drive us to distraction and despair. We moan and cry; yet for the Christian there remains a hope that as God leads us into our grief, God will lead us out. The faithful testimony of God's people is that God accompanies us into and out of sorrow. Jesus seems to be drawn to our grief like a nail to a magnet. He tells us not to be troubled, that he will be with us always, and that God's grace is enough for us.

In his brief sojourn as a pilgrim upon this earth, Jesus explored the depths of the human condition and tasted the bitter wine of human grief and miseries, serving as a model for our response to grief. Out of the depths of his grief Jesus confessed, "I am deeply troubled." Jesus was fully human and fully God; that he was aggrieved teaches us that grief is a part of the human experience, from the trauma of birth until the trauma of our dying.

Most people who are experiencing grief seek to find a way out of their pain. Friends and family may try to coax the mourner out of grief with well-intended but meaningless assertions like, "There, there, we know how much you hurt, but she is in heaven now, waiting for you. You will see her again someday," which the grieving person receives as nonsense. It is *this day* that the hurting soul is enduring; it is the *now* of loss, loneliness, and misery that aches so deeply. Grief hurts! It

Scripture

Brothers and sisters, we want you to know about people who have died so that you won't mourn like others who don't have any hope. Since we believe that Jesus died and rose, so we also believe that God will bring with him those who have died in Jesus.

1 Thessalonians 4:13-14

hurts to the core. A visible display of profound grief can be so frightening that would-be comforters attempt to hush the mourner.

No one can feel the grief and pain of another. No one can get into or under the skin of a grieving soul. Lewis gets very close as he honestly describes his grief. He permits us to see his tears, hear his sobs, and overhear his dialogue with God as he tries to withstand an overwhelming flood of sorrow.

C. S. Lewis wrote frankly and eloquently about his grief. After the death of his wife, Helen Joy Lewis, he expressed most poignantly his thoughts and emotions about this loss. *A Grief Observed* is his account of a grief that may have seemed to him to be like no other; yet it can console others with a sense that someone else understands how they feel. In many notebooks he recorded his anguish; through that processing he gained deeper understandings of life and of death. Here, as in every experience of life, Lewis learned to trust in God.

The testimony of God's suffering people is that God walks with us as we enter into and emerge from our grief. When our grief is overpowering and God seems absent, we can yet give this witness: sometimes when God is most near to us, we may not see God nor taste God's mercy. In spite of its painful wound, grief is nevertheless transitory. The apostle Paul challenges, "Where is your victory, Death? Where is your sting, Death?" (1 Corinthians 15:55).

Out of the grief that consumed him, Lewis eventually emerged more vitalized, focused, and prolific. Lewis learned, as the apostle Paul experienced, God's assurance that "my grace is enough for you, because power is made perfect in weakness" (2 Corinthians 12:9).

18

Faith

Spiritual Reading

To believe that God—at least *this* God—exists is to believe that you as a person now stand in the presence of God as a Person. What would, a moment before, have been variations in opinion, now become variations in your personal attitude to a Person. You are no longer faced with an argument which demands your assent, but with a Person who demands your confidence.

The World's Last Night and Other Essays

On Faith

Rueben Job

Faith is a many-faceted concept. By faith, we often mean fidelity, obedience to, and radical trust in God. Or, we may mean right doctrine or belief about God. C. S. Lewis makes these distinctions and others as he explores the meaning of faith for the person seriously engaged in thinking about or practicing Christianity.

Lewis was one of the most passionate seekers of God and defenders of faith in its several meanings. His own robust faith was reflected in his conversations with colleagues, his teaching, his writing, and his life itself. All served to invite others to engage in faith exploration that was never satisfied with glib or easy answers. To enter this journey of faith, as Lewis did, was to be assured of challenge, struggle, and reward.

Of all the stories, conditions, and claims found in the Scriptures, perhaps none are so mysterious as those made of the power of faith to bring astounding results. When Jesus calmed the stormy sea and asked the terrified disciples about the absence of their faith (Luke 8:22-25), he was speaking of the kind of faith Lewis identifies in his second meaning noted above. Clearly, Jesus was seeking more than intellectual assent to the reality of God's existence. Jesus was seeking the radical trust that comes from consistent experiences of living with God in obedience and trust day after day. Only one who had such faith could have the courage to ask God to calm the seas.

I recently attended Sunday morning worship services with fifteen hundred others. The guest preacher that day was a young woman who was serving as a missionary in Brazil.

In the course of her sermon she spoke about having raised five men from the dead before coming to the United States. After the service, I circulated among the large crowd of worshippers inquiring into their responses to the preacher's claims of raising people from death.

The responses to my inquiry ranged from surprise to downright disbelief. A few, however, mused that such miracles might still occur in Brazil, but they found it quite impossible to believe that such things might happen in their church in Southern California.

The claims of the young woman put everyone to the test that day. In the final analysis, however, she may have been the most honorable of all. Perhaps she would be commended by Jesus, who shortly after raising Lazarus from the dead declared, "I assure you that whoever believes in me will do the works that I do. They will do even greater works than these because I am going to the

Scripture

"I assure you that if you have faith the size of a mustard seed, you could say to this mountain, 'Go from here to there,' and it will go. There will be nothing that you can't do."

Matthew 17:20

Father. I will do whatever you ask for in my name, so that the Father can be glorified in the Son. When you ask me for anything in my name, I will do it" (John 14:12-14).

"I will do whatever you ask for in my name," Jesus says in the above verse. After a while these promises seem to sound like a broken record. It is not that we haven't heard the promises of Jesus; it is that we have "overheard" them. Such audacious claims no longer stop us in our tracks and send chills up our spine.

Nonetheless, Jesus certainly had a great deal to say about the topic of faith. Jesus was that broken record on his assertion that faith works miracles far beyond our wildest expectations. So, if our faith does not "work" for us, what is the cause of the breakdown? Are our expectations too great or too puny? In light of the promises Jesus makes to us, the answer can only be that we have not yet learned or cared to access the awesome promises God extends to us regarding the efficacy of faith. Jesus tells us that even a tiny bit of faith can move mountains—yet we cannot move a molehill.

The plain truth is that we are a long way removed from the faith of the author of Hebrews, who says:

> What more can I say? I would run out of time if I told you about Gideon, Barak, Samson, Jephthah, David, Samuel, and the prophets. Through faith they conquered kingdoms, brought about justice, realized promises, shut the mouths of lions, put out raging

fires, escaped from the edge of the sword, found strength in weakness, were mighty in war, and routed foreign armies. Women received back their dead by resurrection. Others were tortured and refused to be released so they could gain a better resurrection. But others experienced public shame by being taunted and whipped; they were even put in chains and in prison. They were stoned to death, they were cut in two, and they died by being murdered with swords. They went around wearing the skins of sheep and goats, needy, oppressed, and mistreated. The world didn't deserve them. They wandered around in deserts, mountains, caves, and holes in the ground. All these people didn't receive what was promised, though they were given approval for their faith. God provided something better for us so they wouldn't be made perfect without us (Hebrews 11:32-40).

It seems that God might not have necessarily gone to such extremes to provide the early Christians with something better. But the truth remains, the early Christians could have packed their bags and gone home, but they didn't! Rather, they chose to put their faith in the promises God had made to them, and they soon learned that faith is costly, at times terribly so. They moved from faith as agreement to doctrinal beliefs to radical trust and obedience in God and God's way.

Have you ever noticed that a favorite line of the Son of Man is "do not be afraid"? He really must mean it, else he would not remind us so often. But these few words are generally not enough to assuage our fears. And so we assent in our heads while demurring in our hearts: small wonder that Jesus asked his disciples, "Why are you afraid, you people of weak faith?" (Matthew 8:26). Sooner or later, faith puts us to the test. We are to be faithful in the sense of belief, radical trust, and obedience. Apart from this we may miss the blessed inheritance that is ours as children of God and may end our journey of faith as triflers with life's most precious gift.

19

The Holy Spirit

Spiritual Reading

The Lion opened his mouth, but no
sound came from it; he was breathing
out, a long warm breath; it seemed to
sway all the beasts as the wind sways
a line of trees. . . . Then there came
a swift flash like fire (but it burnt
nobody) either from the sky or from
the Lion itself, and every drop of
blood tingled in the children's bodies,
and the deepest, wildest voice they
had ever heard was saying: "Narnia,
Narnia, Narnia, awake. Love. Think.
Speak. Be walking trees. Be talking
beasts. Be divine waters."

The Magician's Nephew

On the Holy Spirit

Perry Bramlett

It would help us all a great deal to remember that in talking about the Spirit, we are talking about the virtual personality of God: a living part of God that acts on, with, and in the human personality. The plain teaching of Holy Scripture is that God's Spirit is always with the Christian and helps us *be* Christian and provides tangible help in the actual, day-to-day living of life. And in a very real sense, the Spirit of God is responsible for our faith. To paraphrase J. B. Phillips, the simple heart of the Christian faith is that our relationship with God is not obedience to an external, other-worldly deity, but a willingness to recognize and be led by God's Spirit within us. When we pray, when we take a "leap of faith," when we show love and honest compassion, when we hunger and thirst after God's Word, when we have patience—these constitute evidence that the Spirit is at work in our lives. God's Holy Spirit does not speak verbally to us, does not work in the arena of the mysterious, and does not show itself in ways known only to television evangelists.

The Spirit is not an impersonal power, yet we cannot expect it to work in the same way or place every time. The Spirit uses us, not the other way around. God moves and works through the Spirit according to God's own creativity, and we must accept the fact that his thoughts and ways are higher than our own. We can know that the Spirit is at work by the good that is done and the love that is shown. When our love begins to be sacrificial, when it begins to be unselfish, when we begin to see and act toward all people as part of God's loved creation, we are demonstrating the greatest indication of the working of the Spirit.

Another important point to remember is that the Spirit helps us in our limitations, perhaps particularly in the area of communication with God. Many people want to pray, hope they will be able to pray, and believe that they are inadequate in prayer. In Romans 8:26-28, Paul spells out clearly the remedy for these limitations. When we do not know how to pray, or do not think we use the right words, the Spirit prays as our substitute. In essence, the Spirit transforms our wish to pray and expresses our deepest questions and longings to God, questions and longings we cannot express. And the Christian God, who knows all things, understands our intentions (which are the most important to him) through the Spirit.

It is interesting that C. S. Lewis did not write much explicitly about the Spirit, as compared to how frequently he examined theological and doctrinal topics as well as God and Jesus. But he often wrote implicitly about the

Scripture

When Pentecost Day arrived, they were all together in one place. Suddenly a sound from heaven like the howling of a fierce wind filled the entire house where they were sitting. They saw what seemed to be individual flames of fire alighting on each one of them. They were all filled with the Holy Spirit and began to speak in other languages as the Spirit enabled them to speak.

Acts 2:1-4

Spirit. In his overall view of this person of the Trinity, Lewis showed a balanced, biblical, traditional outlook, one which we are wise to consider. He wrote several times that Christians should not be worried if they had a vague or "shadowy" notion of the Spirit. He said that we should think of the Spirit as something within or behind us, and that it would be an error to presume that the Spirit spoke or acted *only* within the limits of our own personality. But he also implied that the Spirit, as one author put it in similar words, is capable of "reviving our whole personality." He maintained that the Spirit often works through and is understood (sometimes in hindsight) through the Bible, the church, Christian friends, books, and other things. For Lewis, the Spirit was working most often when a person could feel and sense it least.

In his famous sermon "The Weight of Glory," Lewis spoke with great conviction about how God expects all Christians to act toward others. He went on to say emphatically that the Christian must love everyone with a "real and costly love," just as if we truly believed it.

This type of supernatural love is a gift of the Holy Spirit, the greatest and most desirable gift of all. Can we have this evidence of the Spirit in our lives? Can we learn to see that no one created by God is ordinary? Our answer and our hope always must be yes, and it is good news indeed that the Spirit is right behind and beside us, urging us on, sometimes using exciting and difficult and unexplainable ways. All God wants is our good intentions.

20

Forgiveness

Spiritual Reading

You surely don't mean "feeling that
we are not *worthy* to be forgiven"? For
of course we aren't. Forgiveness by its
nature is for the unworthy. You mean
"Feeling that we *are not* forgiven."
I have known that. I "believed"
theoretically in the divine forgiveness
for years before it really came home to
me. It is a wonderful moment when it
does.

Letters to an American Lady

On Forgiveness

Rueben Job

Forgiveness lies very close to the heart of Christian belief and practice. Remove forgiveness from our theology and what is left is deeply wounded. Remove forgiveness from our practice and our faithfulness is betrayed, our salvation denied, and our hope of community destroyed.

These are the conditions and the reality that we confess every time we pray as Jesus taught us to pray. It is true that for many forgiveness is taken lightly but not for those who have seriously considered their own need of forgiveness and the words of Jesus that link our need with our willingness to forgive. Those who have received genuine forgiveness and those who have given it know both the grace and the cost of this gift. For them forgiveness can never be taken lightly again. Forgiveness is indeed a life-and-death matter.

C. S. Lewis explored the theme of forgiveness at many levels of thought and experience, but all seem to be anchored in the prayer of Jesus, "Forgive us for the ways we have wronged you, just as we also forgive those who have wronged us" (Matthew 6:12). And at no time did Lewis take the concept lightly or suggest that it was easy.

Forgiveness can seem like a fine practice, he says in *Mere Christianity*—until we are faced with the evils committed during times of war. Those who offer forgiveness to an enemy of the state will most likely be branded as unpatriotic. And those who forgive the sins of another may be declared soft and unrealistic. But the forgiveness that Jesus spoke about and Lewis sought to understand and practice is neither soft nor unpatriotic. Forgiveness is not only a preposterous gift but also tremendously difficult and costly. That may be why we talk about it easily but practice it so infrequently.

While Lewis believed that forgiveness must be extended to our enemies, he did not believe that sin should go unpunished. Perhaps it was this concept that made it possible for him to observe that war is a "dreadful thing," but sometimes a Christian is called to wage war. This concept may be helpful to many in a time when terrorism is simmering around the globe. Today faithful persons of all persuasions wonder how to respond to such a vicious and random horror.

The radical nature of forgiveness is seen in the necessity to love and desire good for the enemy, which Lewis also commends. This is not easy to do when the enemy has committed horrendous crimes, taken those we love, destroyed our property, and threatened our way of life. The

Scripture

And whenever you stand up to pray, if you have something against anyone, forgive so that your Father in heaven may forgive you your wrongdoings.

Mark 11:25

way of love, the way of Jesus, demands just this kind of response. To follow Jesus and adopt his values as our own is to love our enemies and desire their good, even when they inflict pain, suffering, and the deaths of those we love. Again, Lewis would not deny punishment of those who commit such crimes, but he was also convinced we must love, desire good, and seek the redemption of even those who seek our destruction. This is the way of living that Jesus taught and practiced.

Forgiveness does not deny the fearful reality or the costly consequences of sin. As a matter of fact, forgiveness takes sin very, very seriously. Sin cannot be brushed aside, overlooked, hidden, or condoned and thought of no consequence. To say that sin does not matter is to make forgiveness impossible. Forgiveness is possible only when there is genuine and honest recognition of the costly reality of sin. Only then can confession and repentance of sin open the gateway to forgiveness. Prior to these steps, forgiveness is impossible and irrelevant. Only after recognition, confession, and repentance can a person accept forgiveness, Lewis says in *The Problem of Pain*.

The alcoholic who recognizes the seriousness of the addiction and realizes there is no hope of recovery without the intervention of God has already taken the first step toward that recovery. To recognize my helplessness is to move toward the possibility of confession and forgiveness. Until I acknowledge the horror of my own sin, I am unable to ask for or accept the forgiveness that God offers through unconditional love. Ownership and responsibility for my own sin are necessary if I am to confess my sin and ask for forgiveness.

Blaming circumstances or others just won't do. I am the one responsible and only I can confess, turn away from sin, and seek forgiveness. Christians need to remind one another often of their responsibility to own up to their own sins. This reminder will help us to offer and receive this gift of love. And finally, we are called to remind each other and the world of God's desire to wipe away the failures and sins of the past and to restore us to that original image of God within us all.

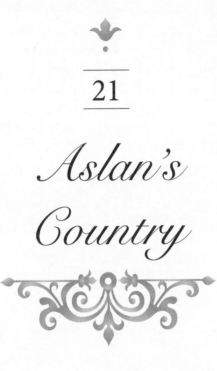

21

*Aslan's
Country*

Spiritual Reading

"Aslan?" said Mr. Beaver, "Why, don't you know? He's the King. He's the Lord of the whole wood, but not often here, you understand. . . . It is he, not you, that will save Mr. Tumnus. . . .

"He'll put all to rights as it says in an old rhyme in these parts:

> Wrong will be right, when Aslan
>   comes in sight,
> At the sound of his roar, sorrows
>   will be no more,
> When he bares his teeth, winter
>   meets its death,
> And when he shakes his mane, we
>   shall have spring again."

*The Lion, the Witch,
and the Wardrobe*

On Aslan's Country

Norman Shawchuck

C. S. Lewis will likely be most remembered for his children's stories. Few authors in modern times have so well succeeded in teaching Christianity to children as has Lewis. He did so by making serious theological tenets understandable and appealing to children. To help him in this endeavor, Lewis recruited the most gentle and ferocious lion in all of Narnia to teach and entice children. Aslan lives in the land of Narnia, a world that only the children and the childlike dare enter.

Lewis took much time to be with children by way of his writing, in which he treated his young pen pals as though they were capable of understanding adult realities. And because he observed the children as mature, the children responded to him in like manner.

In a letter written to a group of fifth graders (printed in his *Letters to Children*), Lewis addressed the subject of living with Aslan (the lion who is the Christ figure in the Narnia series) and how it is that we finally make our way to Aslan's country. Lewis responded, with an admission that he did not know for sure, that the final opening to Aslan's country is through death. However, it is possible, he said, that people who are very good to others may get a glimpse before then.

Having addressed the topic of death, Lewis then turned to their questions about Reepicheep and Nick-a-brick, two more characters from the Narnia stories. Reepicheep was a good mouse, while Nick-a-brick was "worldly oriented." While these two do not represent anyone specific, Lewis told the children, those who are devoted to seeking heaven are like Reepicheep, and those who want some worldly thing so much as to use evil to obtain it are like Nick-a-brick. (Yes, Reepicheep did get to Aslan's country, Lewis confirmed for them.)

An especially appealing aspect of Lewis's interactions with children is that he did not water down his theology or his spirituality for them. He obviously felt that the burden for their understanding was his, not theirs. Thus, he wrote and spoke to them poetically—and candidly. Moreover, he often used his most beloved character, Aslan, as his spokesperson.

Among the most poignant of his letters to his young pen pals are those in which Lewis touched on his own personal life. In one such letter, dated April 23, 1957, Lewis spoke about his wife's illness, saying that Aslan would know best whether to let Joy stay with Lewis or to take her to Aslan's country; but if she were to leave, Lewis would

Scripture

Now we see a reflection in a mirror; then we will see face-to-face. Now I know partially, but then I will know completely in the same way that I have been completely known.

1 Corinthians 13:12

be very sad. By reading his later letters, we begin to realize that there came a point beyond which Lewis experienced Aslan as almost a real expression of God. In a letter to a boy named Laurence, Lewis wrote that though he had been worried about his wife's illness, she was growing stronger and that "Aslan has done great things for us."

In her early teens our youngest daughter, Kay Marie, fell head over heels in love with Lewis's writings. Kay had a much-loved chihuahua, frail and timid at its birth. Kay named her dog Aslan. After many wonderful years, Kay's Aslan died, a few minutes before she arrived for a trip home from college.

That night I wrote in my journal, "Kay's beloved Aslan has got into heaven, a few minutes before she arrived to bid him farewell. Now 'Aslan-the-Small' waits to introduce Kay to 'Aslan-the-Great.' Kay's Aslan was indeed a lionheart; he loved Kay and always will. Other small and great deaths will visit our home along the way; these too are essential to prepare our souls for that awesome moment when Aslan-the-Small introduces Kay to Aslan-the-Great—the Lion Heart of C. S. Lewis."

As a master of fantasy, Lewis was at his very best when writing for children. And by writing for children Lewis captured the imagination of adults as well. By doing so he has secured his place for generations to come as one of the modern world's most brilliant apologists of the Christian faith, who took us along on his journey from atheism to theism to Christianity.

22

The Hope
of Heaven

Spiritual Reading

Heaven can mean (1) The unconditioned Divine Life beyond all worlds. (2) Blessed participation in that Life by a created spirit. (3) The whole Nature or system of conditions in which redeemed human spirits, still remaining human, can enjoy such participation fully and forever. This is the Heaven Christ goes to "prepare" for us. (4) The physical Heaven, the sky, the space in which Earth moves.

Miracles

On the Hope of Heaven

Perry Bramlett

A modern author wrote that the pictures that many Christian writers paint of heaven are often limited and tend to be insipid and dull. It might be added that the images of heaven we hear from the pulpit are the same. Perhaps because of this, some modern people (including Christians) view heaven as a place where no sensible human being would want to go, except for perhaps a brief visit. Who would want to spend all eternity sitting on a cloud playing a harp? Another Christian writer confessed that early on he did not want to go to heaven but simply wanted to escape hell; heaven was "fire insurance." He also had been taught that heaven was a place where we could worship God forever, and since his model for worship was his own church, his mental image of heaven was "Reverend Cant droning on for ever and ever."

It is a sad truth that the limitations of our perceptions of heaven have created problems for many sincere Christians who have simply been repelled by visions of being "stuck in static, unchanging, eternal bliss." In many people's imaginations their picture of heaven is little more than a lampoon, peopled by quaint saints and cherubs and looking vaguely like a giant church. The great Methodist preacher Leslie Weatherhead once said wryly that he wished to be delivered from a heaven that is like an endless church service, and if he or his friends would be singing in the heavenly choir it would not be heaven for anyone.

At least part of the bad theology and teaching about heaven may come from the temptation to fill in the blanks left by the New Testament's not telling us as much as we may want to know about heaven. But it does offer some hints and glimpses. Paul presages several times J. B. Phillips's saying that there will be no VIPs in heaven when the apostle identifies heaven as a gift from God. The author of the Book of Revelation affirmed this in verse 4:10 by saying that the elders will throw down their crowns (relinquish their status) in front of God's throne—in other words, everyone will be equal in heaven. Revelation gives us other hints about the nature of heaven, particularly about its size (large, spacious, and room for all; chapter 21) and its occupants (from all nations and peoples; chapter 7).

There are more glimpses of heaven for us from other parts of the New Testament. Paul, in 2 Corinthians 5:1, tells us that heaven is eternal, unlike earth, which will be torn down. When we look at the big picture in the

Book of Revelation, we see a very persuasive portrait of a heaven that is not only a place of worship and praise, but also a place of service with no limitations. There will be no grief, tears, or mourning and nothing that cuts off, hinders, limits, impedes, or holds back.

Although Jesus did not say that much about heaven, what he did say provides us with some fascinating clues. In Matthew's and Luke's Gospels he tells us (as Paul did later) that the kingdom of God is eternal and indestructible and that it in some way will be similar to an eternal party or banquet. And he also told his disciples that he was going to prepare a place for them and that it would be ready when they got there; he was going on ahead and would meet them there. In these words, Jesus gave us the key to understanding heaven, and from them comes the one word that perhaps describes it best: *community*. Heaven will be a place of fellowship and community, a place where, as one writer put it, "if you like people you will like heaven." This idea was affirmed by Thomas Merton, when he wrote in *The New Seeds of Contemplation* that the true joy a Christian will have in heaven will be the "contemplation of God, if you are there to share it with me." Heaven is a place of shared community, a fellowship with God that is an eternal banquet of delights.

It stands to reason that if heaven is a place of community, it will also be a place of change and growth. In his delightful book *Heaven: The Heart's Deepest Longing*, author Peter Kreeft proposes that eternity is not boring

Scripture

I believe that the present suffering is nothing compared to the coming glory that is going to be revealed to us. The whole creation waits breathless with anticipation for the revelation of God's sons and daughters. . . . And it's not only the creation. We ourselves who have the Spirit as the first crop of the harvest also groan inside as we wait to be adopted and for our bodies to be set free. We were saved in hope. If we see what we hope for, that isn't hope. Who hopes for what they already see? But if we hope for what we don't see, we wait for it with patience.

Romans 8:18-19, 23-25

changelessness (which is limited), because changelessness means that time passes while nothing changes. And he compared heaven to Rivendell, the elven refuge in J. R. R. Tolkien's *The Fellowship of the Ring*: "Time doesn't pass here; it just *is*. A remarkable place altogether!"

Why did Jesus not tell us more about heaven? No one knows for sure. Perhaps because no human words can describe heaven, where life will be so radically different from ours as to defy the imagination, let alone description. But we do have hints and glimpses, and these give us enough light to find our way. And if we were to see or understand heaven in its most complete sense, would we then be able to tolerate the limited and sin-filled world in which we now live?

Although some Christian writers have pictured heaven as limited, bland, and dull, some have described the "place beyond all imagination" in beautiful prose that nudges our imaginations and fills us with wonder. We are so affected by these classic works: *The City of God* (St. Augustine), *The Divine Comedy* (Dante), *Paradise Lost* and *The Pilgrim's Progress* (John Milton), as well as *Phantastes* and *Lilith* (George MacDonald). Perhaps the most perceptive writer about heaven was Lewis, particularly in *The Pilgrim's Regress* (his first explicitly Christian work), *The Great Divorce*, several volumes in the Narnian series, "The Weight of Glory" (his most famous sermon), the chapter "Hope" in *Mere Christianity*, and the chapter "Heaven" (his earliest essay about heaven) in *The Problem of Pain*. He had very little interest in a life after death during the time of his conversion and for about a year afterward. He later counted this a blessing as he knew he had not been enticed into the Christian faith by a promise of heaven.

As Lewis matured as a Christian, he discounted two popular misunderstandings about heaven. One was the informal view that considered heaven too lightly, such as seeing it as a club where friends get together and chat. He also disagreed with those who said that the biblical descriptions of heaven were to be taken literally. He came to believe that the biblical word pictures that associated heaven with earthly riches and splendors (gold, jewels, crowns, musical instruments, and so on) were symbolical attempts by the inspired biblical writers to express the inexpressible.

In "The Weight of Glory," Lewis maintained that no one can enter heaven except in a childlike way, and he compared the obedient child basking in the praise of his parent to the Christian in heaven enjoying the praise of God. And in his compelling fantasy *The Great Divorce* (modeled after *The Divine Comedy*), Lewis sketched a fascinating picture of people in hell who are allowed to visit the outskirts of heaven. If they choose, they can stay in heaven or return to hell, and most choose not to stay. Lewis used this idea to emphasize that we choose our eternal destinies, and that by our choices here on earth we are preparing ourselves for one or the other of the two places.

In *The Last Battle*, Lewis illustrated why the hope of heaven was crucial to his spirituality. He showed heaven as a beautiful continuation of this life, which he called the Shadowlands. Near the end of the story, Narnia has died and frozen over in blackness. The children begin mourning but realize they are walking in a new Narnia, a "different" Narnia where everything is more vibrant and alive than before. The new Narnia is a deeper, richer country, where everything in it seems to have more meaning. Lewis here described his vision of the hope of heaven, "where every chapter is better than the one before."

Lewis knew that heaven is where real life truly begins. He also believed that human beings are created by God with a longing for heaven and are meant to enjoy it as something that is so wonderful that it can only be imagined. His thoughts must have echoed those of the poet John Donne, who wrote, "I shall not live till I see God, and when I have seen him I shall never die."

23

Spirituality in Nature

Spiritual Reading

To shrink back from all that can be
called Nature into negative spirituality
is as if we ran away from horses instead
of learning to ride.

Miracles

On Spirituality in Nature

Norman Shawchuck

The Bible begins by declaring, "In the beginning when God created the heavens and the earth . . ." (Genesis 1:1 NRSV). With this litany of God's creative acts, we are introduced to the spirituality of creation. Everything that God created, and creates, is formed of God's nature. Thus, God who is Spirit endows nature with its own spirituality. The spirituality of God is first to love and to create. We therefore observe that God's initial creations were good, created out of the very nature of the Godhead.

C. S. Lewis had no doubt about the spiritual content of nature. It is a consequence of being created by God. And it was in nature that Lewis found many of the insights about life that found their way into his writing for children and adults. And yet, Lewis was clear that our theology needs more than the natural world as text.

You will recall this famous line from Alfred, Lord Tennyson: nature is "red in tooth and claw." Lewis no doubt understood that predation and violence are part of the natural world. However, he chose to observe human, animal, and plant life from a different perspective. He says in *The Four Loves* that nature tells us to "look, listen, attend." Even a cursory reading of Lewis's writing convinces us that he did look, listen, attend, and therefore drew much of his spirituality from nature, especially the living creatures large and small.

Lewis drew much of his spirituality by observing the behaviors of the creatures that lived inside and outside his home. Among the menagerie of creatures for which Lewis provided food and shelter, and from which he drew great insights, were mice (two of which he named Reepicheep and Nick-a-brick), rabbits, dogs, cats, birds, donkeys, guinea pigs, and hamsters, plus the birds that were wont to visit Lewis in his home. Lewis gained from these creatures an insight into an understanding of spirituality in nature.

First and foremost among Lewis's mythical and real creatures must be, of course, Aslan, a most magnificent (and fictitious) lion, whom Lewis used as a Christ figure in much of his writing. Through Aslan and other creatures living or fictitious, Lewis expressed his own spirituality, one that in many ways was grounded in what he saw in nature.

Lewis once wrote a letter to his brother, Warren, to tell him that Peter, his pet mouse, had barely survived an encounter with a Big Black Cat. He told Warren that the housemaid heard Peter howling and that she came into the room just in time to save Peter's life.

Scripture

But ask Behemoth, and he will teach you,
the birds in the sky, and they will tell you;
or talk to earth, and it will teach you;
the fish of the sea will recount it for you.
Among all these, who hasn't known
that the LORD's hand did this?
In whose grasp is the life of every thing,
the breath of every person?

Job 12:7-10

I understand his concern about the animal in peril. I was born and raised on a ranch in North Dakota. My father and mother treated all of our animals with great respect, and many of them were dearly loved. One of the most beloved was a sheep that as a lamb was very sickly. Our neighbor gave me the feeble lamb soon after its birth, no doubt expecting it would die within a fortnight. My mother put the poor little creature in the kitchen and bottle-fed it to health. The lamb became a huge sheep.

Winter came to the prairie, and on a cold and wet night I acted in a way that made me a recipient of my father's grace. My paternal grandfather was living with us on the ranch, and he and I slept in the same upstairs room. Late at night I heard my sheep calling above the wind and could not resist checking on him. I sneaked down the stairs and out of the house and coaxed my sheep up the stairway and put him in bed with my grandfather and me: snow, ice, mud, and all. Before the family awakened, I led him out of the house to be with the other animals. I thought everything had gone perfectly!

Later that morning, when we gathered around the breakfast table, all was serene until my grandfather laid down his spoon and loudly announced, "Boy! If you ever put that sheep in bed with me again I will kill it!" My mother nearly fainted. My father said not a word, and in that moment I had my first realization of the meaning of grace.

Years later I was introduced to Lewis's works and

realized that his spirituality was nourished by the living things in nature. His writing clarified for me that my own spirituality is formed by nature, and as I walk upon my beloved prairie, I come to realize this is not "where" I am; it is "who" I am. I and my spirituality are grounded in nature.

24

The Heart of a Child

Spiritual Reading

Children are not deceived by fairy-tales;
they are often and gravely deceived by
school-stories. Adults are not deceived
by science-fiction; they can be deceived
by the stories in the women's magazines.

A Mind Awake

On the Heart of a Child

Norman Shawchuck

That Lewis loved children and young people becomes clear when one reviews the many letters he wrote to them in England and the United States. Lewis maintained writing relationships with several young people on both continents. He served as a spiritual director to many children, though they might not have realized that.

The last letter Lewis wrote was to one of his pen pals, a young lad named Philip, dated November 22, 1963. Lewis praises Philip's fine writing skills and goes on to address the boy's interest in the Narnia series. He notes that children have no trouble discerning who Aslan the lion represents, yet grown-ups always seem blind to that.

One of these young people was Laurence, a boy from America. Lewis assures Laurence that he understands the boy's struggling to maintain a belief in the afterlife and encourages him to consider also the difficulty of comprehending no afterlife. He then tells Laurence about a little bird who flew into Lewis's home and spent the night there. In the morning, a student who worked in Lewis's home

Scripture

At that time the disciples came to Jesus and asked, "Who is the greatest in the kingdom of heaven?"

Then he called a little child over to sit among the disciples, and said, "I assure you that if you don't turn your lives around and become like this little child, you will definitely not enter the kingdom of heaven. Those who humble themselves like this little child will be the greatest in the kingdom of heaven. Whoever welcomes one such child in my name welcomes me."

Matthew 18:1-5

captured the bird and gently returned it outside, where it reunited with its mother. Lewis left the letter there, but one can imagine that the child pondered its meaning for himself, and perhaps his spirituality was formed a bit more through a consideration of God's nature.

By observing and interacting with animals, Lewis also saw how God was present and active in the world. Children related to his interest in animals. Lewis wrote to his goddaughter: "I must tell you what I saw in a field—one young pig crossed the field with a great big bundle of hay in its mouth and deliberately laid it down at the feet of an old pig. I could hardly believe my eyes. I'm sorry to say that the old pig didn't take the slightest notice. Perhaps it couldn't believe its eyes either" (*Letters to Children*).

Of course, he believed the Genesis story—that humans were created in the image of God—and discussed this with children as well. In a letter to a child named Hugh, he says, "In general, I incline to think that tho' the blessed will participate in the Divine Nature, they will do so always in a mode which does not simply annihilate their humanity. Otherwise it is difficult to see why the species were created at all. Of course I'm only guessing" (*Letters to Children*).

Lewis took children seriously. He responded to them not with condescension but with genuine respect for their thoughts, concerns, and relationships to God. He gave them no less than his best attention. If we truly wish to develop discipleship in children, we would do well to emulate Lewis's way of relating to them.

25

The Church
and Sacraments

Spiritual Reading

Our life as Christians begins by being
baptised into a death; our most joyous
festivals begin with, and centre upon,
the broken body and the shed blood.

Reflections on the Psalms

On the Church
and Sacraments

Perry Bramlett

A book about C. S. Lewis published in the 1990s declared that he was "a Christian for all Christians." Another book published a few years later said that a primary reason for his appeal was his ecumenicity, or appeal to all Christians. This is a prominent theme in Lewis's book *Mere Christianity*. He was a member of the Anglican Church, but he was not an ordained clergyperson; nor did he ever work in any capacity for the church. In his preface to *Mere Christianity*, Lewis warned the reader that he was not offering aid to anyone who was hesitating between denominations, nor was he trying to convert anyone to his own position; rather, he was attempting to explain and defend the belief that "has been common to nearly all Christians at all times." He also stated that he was an ordinary layman of the Church of England, not especially "high" or "low" or "especially anything else." Before *Mere Christianity* was published, it was submitted to four clergy of four denominations (Anglican, Catholic, Methodist, and Presbyterian) for their comments and suggestions.

A few years ago, an American writer visited Oxford, England, and while there visited Lewis's "home church," Holy Trinity. The little church (still an active congregation) stands in the suburb of Headington Quarry, about a mile from Lewis's home, the Kilns. The writer met a kindly warden of the church, and in the course of their conversation, he asked the elderly gentleman about Lewis's worship habits. The man had known Lewis and his brother, Warren, well and remembered that they sat together in the same pew for over thirty years, a pew that now has a commemorative marker attesting to that fact. When asked why Lewis attended this particular church (there were several others nearby), the warden laughed and explained that this was the closest church to Lewis's house. And that he and "Warnie" were always the first to take Holy Communion and the first to leave.

Lewis did not particularly enjoy going to church, and when on holiday, he visited and recommended small churches. He said that he preferred private prayer and meditation, yet he attended several church services each week at his college chapel in Oxford (and later Cambridge) and at Holy Trinity. Most church activities did not appeal to Lewis; the organized institutional parts of it were distracting and a waste of time, he believed.

One reason for his dislike of going to church, aside from its annoying "busyness," was the fact that often the preaching he heard as a young man was boring and uncharitable. He was exposed to the "loveless, graceless" sermons of his grandfather, which consisted primarily of rants and diatribes against Catholicism. After he grew up, he had another problem with church services: many of the theologians and preachers of his day had left orthodoxy behind and insisted on speaking of Jesus as only a great teacher and wise man, and neglected Jesus's divinity and watered down his explicit commands concerning discipleship and witness.

Lewis saw the church universal as an extension of the incarnation of Jesus, the body of Christ that continues to do his work. Christians and the church are literally a part of Christ, he believed, and every new Christian helps Christ accomplish more in the world. Lewis also saw the church as providing the only adequate means for a Christian to learn both about God and how to spread the Christian "good infection," as he called, in *Mere Christianity,* sharing the life of Christ.

One author speculated that Lewis did not write much about the sacraments of the church because of the divisions they had caused. Lewis believed this and thought that Christians of different denominations and outlooks usually emphasized their approach to the sacraments at the expense of at least listening to other views. Lewis did write about communion in his last Christian book, *Letters*

Scripture

When the hour came, he took his place at the table, and the apostles with him. He said to them, "I have eagerly desired to eat this Passover with you before I suffer; for I tell you, I will not eat it until it is fulfilled in the kingdom of God."

Luke 22:14-16 NRSV

to Malcolm. He never really did understand rationally how the taking of wine and bread actually helped him or how it related to the Christian community. But as a longtime reader of the Book of Common Prayer he remembered that it stressed that the regular partaking of communion enables a person to identify with Jesus, provided that person takes it with integrity. For Lewis, integrity meant obeying the commands of Jesus, whether he understood them or not. As he grew older, he came to appreciate Holy Communion and looked forward to taking it. Not only was he obedient to Christ, but he discovered that his soul was often refreshed and nourished through Communion. And he was obedient to the sacrament of baptism as well. He knew that baptism in itself was not the mark of a Christian, nor did it "prove" that one is a follower of Christ. But he saw it as a "magical" (or mysterious) way in which God spreads the Christian life to the world through the body of Christ, the church. And he also knew that baptism was a way, at least in part, that a Christian could identify with, and thus witness to, the life of Christ.

As a traditional Anglican, Lewis favored the use of the liturgy for church prayers. He believed that it was easier to worship when one used the established prayers that stood the test of time and that these were almost always better (and had more integrity) than spontaneous prayers that people made up on the spur of the moment. He did not disapprove of all spontaneous prayer, but in

Letters to Malcolm, he complained that sometimes we do not pray "small prayers," because we place our own dignity ahead of God's dignity. And Lewis knew that the Bible did not condemn repetitions but did admonish against *vain* repetitions. His favored form of prayer was the Lord's Prayer.

It could be said that what Lewis wanted most from a church was a sense of the mystery of God, and he received this most often in small, quiet, traditional churches. Someone has written that the mystery of God is a consciousness of God that does not end no matter how deep we go. The problem for many who want to find or have an experience with God at a church is that their perceptions of God are often too cluttered by the busy routines of the churches they attend. We need to understand and be aware of the holiness of time, and the church that allows for (even occasional) deliberateness, silence, and reflection can remind us of this.

Unless we make the effort to redeem the sacredness of time—in our liturgies, music, preaching, and other activities—we will often not develop any real awareness of it, and we will not use it to listen for and respond to God. In *Letters to Malcolm,* Lewis praised people who attend church services not to be entertained and who object to novelties in worship. Novelty (as well as "busy-ness"), Lewis believed, encourages us to focus on it and the service itself. Thinking about worship is not the same as worshipping, he said. And clergy, even the most well-intentioned, can fall into this trap. Some believe that they should periodically place a new spin on the liturgy or the church service, thinking that will attract visitors and add extra pizazz. Lewis would counter this by saying the church must lead outside of itself to Christ, and when the clergy call attention to themselves, or something they have done, this dilutes and even obliterates the mystery of God and leads only to a surface understanding, if anything at all.

A modern author wrote that our churches often lack "the personality of God." Many of us only know God through Scripture, the lives of others, and events from our own past and, hopefully, from our present. One prominent pastor once complained that he had never encountered God in a church, and he had tried to all of his life. He had read all the Scripture passages, prayed regularly, had many friends who were Christians, and so on. We can keep in mind, however, that knowledge of God does not let us hold God or become intimate with God. When we encounter the mystery of God through liturgy, the sacraments, reflection, and quiet, we bring to God our own darkness, our own deepest needs, and our own desire, however tentative, to be like Christ. Can this happen in church? It possibly can, if we cease to perceive God to be an idea or a teaching or an announcement. It possibly can, if we can understand Christ to be more than just a wise teacher or an extraordinary human being.

Authentic spirituality is our cooperation in the process

that God started when God called us to be Christians; the process by which we become "gods by adoption." Lewis said the same thing but used the phrase "little Christs." And he knew that although the church is not always perfect, authentic spirituality is somehow maintained and mysteriously nourished in it. In the church we can become a little Christ. We can be free to love ourselves and love others. We can become free to use our minds and our talents and our personalities. In the church we can start to become all that we were meant to be. How? That is the mystery.

26

Evangelism

Spiritual Reading

But of course our anxiety about
unbelievers is most usefully employed
when it leads us, not to speculation
but to earnest prayer for them and the
attempt to be in our own lives such
good advertisements for Christianity
as will make it attractive.

Letters of C. S. Lewis

On Evangelism

Perry Bramlett

A well-known clergyperson and writer once conducted an informal survey among the people he spoke to on several occasions, asking them how they came to their salvation or came to know Jesus as their personal savior. He also asked them if they became Christian by listening to a Christian radio or television program or by listening to and responding to a sermon in a church. The total number who replied yes to those three questions was a very small percentage, about 2 or 3 percent of the several thousand respondents. But when he asked them how many had become Christians because a person who cared about them had shared the good news of their experience with Jesus Christ and salvation, the response was overwhelming.

This personal sharing of the good news of Jesus's offer of salvation is called evangelism. The overall view held by most Christian denominations and churches is that the truth of the salvation story should be shared with others and that the events of Christ and his death and resurrection are the gospel, the good news that leads to eternal life. At its best, evangelism is a loving way of making faith a possibility to the world, and it is widely agreed that this good news should be told as well as lived. One of the important features of the Christian faith is that Jesus's story can be expressed in words by almost anyone, just as it can be expressed through the life of a believer.

One author has written that the church (and the individual Christian) must be careful of two possible errors concerning evangelism. One is the danger of treating people as impersonal souls, just names to be added to the church rolls. And some people associate evangelism, witness, and "soul winning" with coercion and high-pressure tactics. A related error may occur when a person (or church), in reaction to coercive and manipulative conversion practices, gives up on evangelism. The church and individual Christian must remember that the early Christian church was characterized by a loving aggressiveness in sharing the good news of the gospel to the world. So, it stands to reason that a positive alternative to these errors would have to include a balance of verbal, personal, accepting, loving, and genuinely caring concern for the individual person.

Some modern approaches to evangelism tend to shy away from personal witness and, while not neglecting it completely, relegate it to a secondary role behind (or perhaps alongside) what might be called the nonverbal, action-oriented approach to evangelism: the living out of the gospel in faithful obedience. In some churches, it seems that discussions of Christian mission or evangelism are pitted against discussions of social action or charity. As one person said, "Some of us tend to be talkers and others of us doers, and the doers are in the majority."

This division is illustrated by an anecdote that has been around for years. A zealous young man was witnessing at a local fast-food store, accosting the patrons as they exited and asking them, "Brother (or sister), are you saved?" and handing them a pamphlet that contained brief instructions on how to be saved. As the story goes, one elderly man did not say a word when approached and instead pulled out a piece of paper, wrote for a few minutes, then handed it to the young man. "These are names of my neighbors and folks I work with," he said. "Ask them if I'm saved."

It seems clear that the best approach to evangelism and witness must be marked with love and that Christians must realize that it is not an art, science, or set program of rigidly adhered-to "laws" and is not the same for everyone. The New Testament (particularly the Book of Ephesians) teaches that evangelism is a gift and that Christians should use their different gifts in the community of the church with cooperation and a sense of respect for others with different gifts. It should also be remembered that in the doing and telling of the gospel, Christians have the great example of Jesus. When pointing

Scripture

There was a man sent from God, whose name was John. He came as a witness to testify to the light, so that all might believe through him. He himself was not the light, but he came to testify to the light.

John 1:6-8 NRSV

people toward God, Jesus taught, preached, listened, accepted, healed, and showed mercy and compassion, and we may say and do as he did. His was the holistic approach to evangelism; he saw people not as souls or statistics but as children of God. His evangelism was both verbal and action-oriented, but his life complemented his message; they balanced each other.

There is no question that C. S. Lewis saw his own evangelistic witness as a gift from God, and how he used it and what he said about it are well worth noting. The Christian world has noted this: he has been labeled as a "teaching evangelist," a "literary evangelist," "the apostle to the skeptics," "the winsome evangelist," and "the evangelist to the modernists." In his Christian works Lewis had three primary objectives. One was to present the Christian faith as he interpreted it to nonbelievers, those "not of the faith." Another was to defend and make a reasoned and intelligible case for the Christian faith for his fellow Christians, particularly those who had questions and doubts. And his third objective was to defend the validity of traditional Christianity, the historic faith that most Christians throughout history have believed and trusted.

Although many of his religious works have helped and are still helping legions of Christians, Lewis was mostly writing to the unbeliever. He strongly believed in a universal moral law created by God and was saddened by the failure of humanity to live up to it. He saw that human beings (including himself), as sinners, had offended God, who had created the universe for good. In *Mere Christianity,* Lewis wrote that although God gave humans a free will, more often than not people would choose bad over good. God had to become human in the person of Jesus in order to save the world and to offer salvation. Lewis wrote several times about the importance of our recognizing our sin and believing in a savior who takes away that sin. This urgent message comes through time and time again in his Christian books, and he said himself that "most of my books are evangelistic."

Lewis believed very strongly in evangelism and thought that every Christian should try in some way to evangelize others. He cautioned often that we must remember that God works in different ways with different people, and it is decidedly wrong to want everyone to conform to a set pattern of witness, especially our own. He also warned that most of the time, it is what we do, rather than what we say, that contributes most effectively to people's salvation. Lewis believed that his gift was in the area of intellectual evangelism rather than the emotional appeal. He once said that the ideal evangelistic team would consist of two people: one to appeal to the emotions and the other to the intellect. He saw that the greatest difficulty of the intellectual approach was keeping the reader's or listener's mind on the truth. Many hearers, Lewis observed, believe that when a speaker recommends Christianity it is because the speaker thinks it is good, not necessarily because it is true.

It is interesting to note that Lewis also saw himself as a translator of evangelistic truth. He believed that many people in his day had not been convinced of the truth and reliability of the claims of Christianity by either a highly emotional appeal or by the often-unintelligible language of preachers or theologians. He wrote his books with that in mind, turning traditional and long-accepted Christian doctrine and theology into the language, the vernacular, that most fairly well-educated people could understand.

One of Lewis's most celebrated works of fantasy is *The Great Divorce*, published in 1945. An often studied (and praised) chapter concerns an apostate bishop who once had good intentions but came to favor the modern and successful and was afraid of the old ideas of "crude salvationism" and authentic spirituality because "they weren't popular anymore." This pastor eventually rejected the offer of heaven in order to attend a meeting and present a paper to a group of clergy! This story is a wonderful vignette and was Lewis's jab at the extreme theological liberalism he sometimes encountered while a professor at Oxford.

It may have also been a subtle tribute to a simple evangelism that produces Christians who may not be theologically astute but nevertheless remain faithful. But Lewis was not naive. He knew that along with basic evangelism there must be sound teaching and preaching. He saw that authentic evangelism has as much to do with the making of disciples (as Jesus commanded) as it has to do with numbers and converts.

It is evident that Lewis was a Christian of strong evangelistic beliefs, and these were among the most important aspects of his spirituality. But he was not a "talking evangelist." His Christian witness demonstrated itself again and again in his teaching, preaching, writing, praying, and mentoring. As we look back and reflect on his life, we can be comforted to know that he was and will always remain a reliable and trustworthy guide.

27

The Grace of Good Books

Spiritual Reading

Literary experience heals the wound,
without undermining the privilege,
of individuality. There are mass
emotions which heal the wound; but
they destroy the privilege. In them
our separate selves are pooled and we
sink back into sub-individuality. But
in reading great literature I become a
thousand men and yet remain myself.
. . . I see with a myriad eyes, but is still
I who see. Here, as in worship, in love,
in moral action, and in knowing, I
transcend myself; and am never more
myself than when I do.

An Experiment in Criticism

On the Grace
of Good Books

Perry Bramlett

The Oxford English Dictionary uses a bouquet of words to describe *grace*, among them *divine favor*, *influence*, *inspiration*, *virtue*, *wholesome* (quality), *impart* (strength), and several others, most having to do with something that is positive, inspirational, and, often, given (by God). The idea of grace offered as a gift was echoed by the well-known Christian author Frederick Buechner (a great admirer of C. S. Lewis), when he wrote that we never *get* grace but that it is something we are given, and that the gift of grace can be ours only if we will reach out and take it.

It has been observed that many modern Christians do not understand or have never been taught that good books and stories are a gift from God and that these can be rightly called signs that reveal God's loving, gift-giving nature. When we read, savor, enjoy, ponder, and learn from good books, we should understand that this (which we should never take for granted) is a very easy way to receive God's gift of grace. All we have to do is visit a bookshop or library and then take the time to read well.

The graces of good books and reading are many. We all know that books and stories can entertain and be fun; they help us escape (at least for a while) from an increasingly stressful world. When we take a night (or even a few hours) off from the television or computer and curl up with a good book or story, we can laugh, be thrilled, and receive hope, often from just one page. Good books also help us understand our world, culture, society, and times, and even ourselves. When we read, we can receive the grace of insight and self-understanding. The best of good reading can present to our minds and hearts not only ideas that are appealing and intellectually and emotionally stimulating, but perhaps those we may want to make our own.

We don't know if C. S. Lewis considered the verse from Matthew's Gospel (above) to be one of his favorites, but a careful reading of his letters, autobiographical works, and the several good biographies about him indicates that it could have been. It has been suggested that it may be the most neglected of all of Jesus's commandments. If anyone ever loved the Lord their God with their *whole* mind, it was Lewis, and his example is a wonderful encouragement for us. He knew that reading good books and stories helps us keep and honor Jesus's commandment, because in reading these we often (and should) use the part of our mind that is creative, imaginative, wondering, and dreaming.

One of Lewis's popular and enduring stories is *The Great Divorce*, a fantasy concerning heaven, hell, and the lifelong choices people make that help send them to either of these two eternal places. Although Lewis cautioned the reader in his preface to not speculate too much about the rational details of the afterlife, a close reading of this entrancing tale does make the reader aware of the possibilities of God and how God often creates and moves and changes, using methods we would not think of rationally. Not long ago, a church group was asked, after a first reading of *The Great Divorce*, what their impressions were. They said they would never think about heaven and hell in the same way again. And many in the group affirmed that they were going to not only read Lewis's story again but also search the Scriptures and "work out their own salvation" as to their beliefs and ideas about ethical choices and right Christian living. Lewis would smile! A good book or story like *The Great Divorce* opens up our imaginations and allows us to wonder and to see things from a new angle. When we love God with our whole mind, we can know firsthand that God does indeed offer his grace in mysterious ways that we would not ordinarily "see" using only our rational facilities.

Two years before his death, Lewis published his only

Scripture

"You must love the Lord your God with all your heart, with all your being, and with all your mind."

Matthew 22:37

book of literary theory, a little masterpiece called *An Experiment in Criticism*. This work is, at its most basic, an encouragement for readers to enjoy good books and stories for what they bring us. Lewis reminds us that if we want to become good readers, we have to surrender to what we are reading, to read it with our whole mind and heart. He wrote that when we do this, our good reading experience will have something in common with love and moral action: we are accepting the book or story without pre-judging it. Lewis stated further that when we read well, we should not be so concerned with whether a book or story is "right" or "wrong" (or whether we do or do not agree with the author), but we should read to understand fully the opinions of others. In this way, we can learn to appreciate books and the ideas and experiences in them for what they are, while at the same time not losing our sense of our own opinions and experiences.

Lewis read not only for instruction and guidance in his vocation of a teacher of English literature but also for pleasure and to experience beauty. It seems he read everything, including classical drama and medieval texts, the great English poets, the English Romantics and Victorians, fantasy and science fiction, philosophy, Christian devotional and theological works (by George MacDonald, G. K. Chesterton, and many others), popular thrillers and classic novels (by James Fenimore Cooper, Leo Tolstoy, Jane Austen, and Charles Williams, for example), and much, much more. He particularly loved the great old children's stories such as the tales of Beatrix Potter, Lewis Carroll's *Alice* stories, *The Wind in the Willows*, and the delightful stories of Edith Nesbit. He urged his friends and correspondents to always reread good books, as he believed that a reader could not fully enjoy a book or story on a first reading. For Lewis, the experience of reading and rereading was similar to an exhilarating journey to a place that is so wonderful the traveler wants to return to it again and again. He wrote several times that only after rereading could one savor and fully take to heart the literary and devotional riches hidden in good books and stories.

Sometimes we forget that books and stories at their best are artistic, and the Christian reader can have the delightful privilege of enjoying their artistry and beauty. A good book depicts for the reader ideas and expressions of beauty, whether it contains a play, stories, novel, or poetry, and these literary genres or types do have elements of the artistic. The unity, design, balance, use of language, and descriptions in a good book or story can enhance our perception of beauty and show us how to best enjoy it. Poorly written books are seldom remembered (except for how bad they are), but those that are well written stay with us longer, sometimes for a lifetime. To paraphrase Lewis, it is easy to forget that the author who wrote a love story needs to know something not only about love but also about writing well. A well-written and crafted story can haunt, charm, sometimes disturb, and nearly always transport us to new experiences of the mind and heart. God created beauty and art, and our lives should be lived in the awareness of that. From a Christian perspective, we should also be mindful that literary artists have created for us expressions of God's beauty, that God wants us to enjoy them, and when we do, we can feel and know God's good pleasure.

Lewis was a reader his entire life. He always appreciated the grace and beauty of good books and stories, as they entertained and inspired him, challenged him to think logically and clearly, and informed him as a devoted Christian who cared deeply about his world. And thanks be to God for continuing to give to us the grace-filled gift of Lewis's good books and stories.

28

Spiritual Direction

Spiritual Reading

One must get over any false shame
about accepting necessary help. One
never *has* been "independent." Always,
in some mode or other, one has lived
on others, economically, intellectually,
spiritually. . . . We are members of
one another whether we choose to
recognise the fact or not.

Letters to an American Lady

On Spiritual Direction

Perry Bramlett

Christian spiritual direction can be defined as the care or guidance of people by advice, counsel, and prayer. A spiritual director may be a clergyperson or experienced layperson, and often a spiritual director sees his or her vocation of direction as a spiritual gift. A spiritual director is like a commonsense doctor of the soul, a wise and experienced person who tries to discern the condition of a person's soul or spiritual life. In an ideal relationship, the spiritual director counsels or teaches people to become more mature Christians, particularly in an authentic understanding of themselves based on their relationship to God and the living of life through faith and prayer. In the best situations, a person who is taught and counseled by a spiritual director learns to love God for who God is, and this leads to a selfless love for one's neighbor and oneself.

But it is important to understand that a spiritual director is more than just a wise teacher or counselor. A spiritual director should also be, at best, a caring friend who encourages with kindness, demonstrates trust in the relationship, and accepts without being judgmental. The spiritual director should also be a person who integrates theory with practice and is a moral and spiritual example in their own lives. In this day and age, when our so-called spiritual leaders are often exposed as having feet (and hearts) of clay, we need spiritual directors who practice what they preach and teach—that is, people who exemplify stability, truth, and wisdom.

Spiritual direction has its roots deep within the early traditions of the church. Since the Reformation, it has relied on confession and dialogue but, at its best, is not authoritarian and inflexible. Spiritual direction should not be followed arbitrarily, and it should be counterbalanced with a person's conscience, the evidence and weight of the teachings of the Bible and the church, common sense, and relevant circumstances. The spiritual director should never be a dictator, and the person being directed should never follow blindly.

Today, we live in an age of increased interest in spirituality, and supreme importance is often placed on spiritual direction and its counterpart: spiritual kinship or mentoring. Self-help groups (such as Alcoholics Anonymous) and books and periodicals abound; psychologists and professional counselors work with lay directors, particularly in the area of vocational and career choice; and churches are more interested than ever in hiring staff

Scripture

What of the wisdom from above? First, it is pure, and then peaceful, gentle, obedient, filled with mercy and good actions, fair, and genuine.

James 3:17

and clergy with counseling and mentoring experience and involving the laity in some type of mentor training. Often a secular spiritual director or mentor is a friend, a person who acts as a guide in regard to a new career, profession, job, or a developmental stage, such as the transition between school and career. Many Christian spiritual directors are clergy, teachers, or experienced Christians who have a reputation for spiritual wisdom.

It is not widely known that C. S. Lewis, perhaps the greatest Christian defender of the faith of the twentieth century, started a weekly practice of confession to a spiritual director, beginning in late 1940. This was a difficult decision for Lewis, as his Anglican tradition practiced general confessions of the congregation at worship services and communion. One problem he encountered with the confessions in the Book of Common Prayer was that they could be as specific or general as one wished. But he read an exhortation for the service of Holy Communion that advised that if a person needed help and counsel in quieting their conscience, they could go to their priest "or some other discreet and learned Minister of God's Word" to receive counsel and advice.

The time around 1940 that Lewis decided to seek spiritual direction was a very difficult one for him. He was about to start work on *The Screwtape Letters*, a book that would become very demanding emotionally, as he had to learn to "think like evil" and bare his own soul and its temptations. He worried about his brother and best friend, Warren, who had been sent to military duty in France. He, like everyone else in Europe, feared an invasion, and the peril of imminent war led to his service in the Home Guard. His wartime radio talks, later published as *Mere Christianity*, served to hasten his involvement in debates about the war, which caused conflict with some of his pacifist friends. His decision to seek out a spiritual director and the discipline required provided him with a faith and guidance that sustained and nourished him and helped him become a mentor himself, to countless people all over the world.

Lewis is a wonderful example for all who seek spiritual direction and for those who give it. He was a spiritual mentor in at least three ways. First, he was a tutor (teacher) to scores of undergraduates who studied at his university (Oxford) for over thirty years. One of his students, Harry Blamires (who later became an effective Christian apologist), said that Lewis knew how to nourish a pupil through encouragement without causing resentment and that he saw himself as a guide who was starting students (especially the responsive ones) on a process of learning that would last the rest of their lives. And many of his students became his friends. One of them, Allan Griffiths, testified that it was through his friendship with Lewis that his mind was gradually brought back to Christianity.

Lewis was also a spiritual director through the ministry of letter-writing, a lost art in our culture of electronic communication. After he became world-famous with the publication of *The Problem of Pain, Mere Christianity, The Screwtape Letters, Miracles,* and other books, he received thousands of letters a year, from all over the world, asking for advice and counsel. Many of his letters have been published, and virtually all show Lewis's pastoral concern as a friend, counselor, and "mere Christian." His letters also exhibit two wonderful characteristics of the authentic spiritual director: his ability to laugh at himself and his willingness to share his life's experiences and spiritual difficulties. These are particularly evident in *Letters to An American Lady,* a record of a mentoring relationship with a widow named Mary Willis Shelbourne, which lasted well over ten years. Lewis's letters to Mary show him encouraging her with serious spiritual advice, often about prayer and learning how to live day by day and not worrying about the future. But he also shared with her the everyday experiences of his own life: anecdotes about his pets, his visits to Ireland, the books he was reading, his marriage, and much more. Lewis demonstrated in these letters (and many others) that authentic spiritual direction is often more than just counsel and talk about religion; it is the friendly and compassionate sharing of one's whole life.

Lewis was also a very effective lay preacher, and this was for him a method of spiritual direction. He was often in great demand as a preacher and spoke in the college chapels of Oxford and Cambridge, in London and other cities, and to the troops during World War II. Several who heard Lewis preach in person have testified that they heard his sermons as personal spiritual guidance. One testified that Lewis always forged a personal bond with those who heard him, and another said that many identified with what Lewis was saying because of his personal attentiveness and obvious concentration on his hearers when he spoke. Lewis preached using the vernacular, the ordinary language of the people, wore a suit instead of a clerical robe, and used everyday stories and anecdotes in his sermons. This was not posturing. Lewis knew he was not a "professional" theologian or a trained, ordained clergyperson. He was, he always insisted, just a "mere Christian," and he was, as one author wrote, "struggling like the rest of his listeners" to understand and make sense of life and the Christian faith. This honest self-appraisal was a key element in his identification with his hearers, and it helped them receive his words as spiritual direction.

Lewis's life as both a spiritual mentor and one who sought direction has implications for us today. First, he was a great friend to many, and the care and concern that go with that are important parts of spiritual direction— perhaps the most important parts. We can learn from him and understand that in spiritual mentoring or direction, true friendship is perhaps the best place from which we should begin. We can also learn from Lewis that mentoring takes many forms and does not necessarily take place in a counselor's office, a church, or other "professional" setting. One can be a spiritual director from the pulpit, from the teaching podium in church school, in letters or e-mail messages, or through a variety of other forms and places. Authentic mentoring is interrelated with all parts of life. Along with this, we can learn from Lewis that spiritual direction does not have to be confined to a one-on-one relationship and that it can be ministered effectively in large groups and non-church settings.

Perhaps the most important idea we can learn from Lewis about spiritual direction is that it is, at its best, a shared relationship. We must be willing to share our whole self with the person we are directing, and this includes our struggles, doubts, and fears. This takes courage, but it will bring us closer to each other, and this closeness will ultimately give birth to community and real spiritual health. And we must take care to remember that spiritual direction is not confined to specific spaces and times. Lewis never visited Mary Willis Shelbourne in America. He never talked to her on the telephone and never corresponded or communicated with anyone who knew her. But they corresponded faithfully, shared their honest feelings, and always reminded each other of their prayers and concern. Through this they became true friends and did meet, as mere Christians.

29

Laughter and the Comic Spirit

Spiritual Reading

But it is immortals whom we joke
with, work with, marry, snub, and
exploit—immortal horrors or
everlasting splendours. This does not
mean that we are to be perpetually
solemn. We must play. But our
merriment must be of that kind (and
it is, in fact, the merriest kind) which
exists between people who have,
from the outset, taken each other
seriously—no flippancy, no superiority,
no presumption.

*The Weight of Glory and
Other Addresses*

On Laughter and the Comic Spirit

Perry Bramlett

Some Christians have problems with the words *comic* and (even) *laughter* when they are used in a religious context, such as in a Christian publication. For some, these words bring to mind comic books or newspaper comic strips or mindless television situation comedies, which many consider to be silly or foolish. And if *comic* and *laughter* are used about the Bible or its contents, some people become very serious indeed and see this as belittling the Holy Scriptures.

If we read the Bible carefully, we will discover that it often pokes fun at us—our pride, pretentiousness, selfishness, greed, and many more of our failings and shortcomings that go far beyond and around the seven deadly sins. The prophets, particularly Isaiah and Amos (and before them, Elijah), poked fun at and ridiculed the false religions and counterfeit worship of the Israelites, along with rebuking the greedy who plundered for their own needs while neglecting the poor. And Jesus himself (most often in his parables) used humorous, biting irony and satire to chastise the hypocrisies of the organized religion of his day and the deadly selfishness of many others who considered themselves righteous.

A few days after C. S. Lewis's death, his longtime and great friend Owen Barfield began to reread several letters he had received from Lewis. After reading two or three, he found himself laughing out loud. Lewis, he said, had a tremendously strong sense of the comic, an irrepressible bent for comedy. Lewis was certainly not a social buffoon or a professional comedian, nor was he (according to Barfield and other friends) openly flippant or trivial. But he was a Christian of laughter and joy, a man who had a cheery heart and disposition, and this outlook on life shined through in many (if not all) of his writings, both academic and Christian. It is no accident that a published volume of his essays is titled *The Joyful Christian*.

Lewis's attitude of laughter is and should be a great example for all of us because we were created by God to laugh. This can be at least partly supported by the fact that children never need to be taught to laugh, but only when *not* to laugh, and it seems that humans are the only animals that *can* laugh. Laughter was given to us by God as a gift, and only God would bestow on his creation something as enjoyable as the comic spirit, the spirit of laughter that releases us from tensions and stress and helps preserve us from our natural inclination to pompousness.

Scripture

Jesus said to his disciples, "I assure you that it will be very hard for a rich person to enter the kingdom of heaven. In fact, it's easier for a camel to squeeze through the eye of a needle than for a rich person to enter God's kingdom."

Matthew 19:23-24

Humor and the comic spirit are also God's gifts for the church, but it seems that there are people in all churches who try to suppress it. One author wrote that when he was having lunch with a friend who was a member of a "small, rather humorless Protestant denomination," the man became angry and walked away from the table when the author suggested that Jesus laughed and enjoyed playing with children. There is also a story about the editor of a Christian periodical who was distressed when he found a place in the New Testament where Jesus *may* have laughed.

It may be a matter of concern that there have been and are few Christian writers who used or now use humor in their work. Only a handful of names come to mind, starting with Lewis and G. K. Chesterton. It seems that many have forgotten, or have never been taught, that the comic spirit is not just a sign of God's presence in our lives but also shows that God's presence invariably (and hopefully) makes us want to laugh for sheer joy. God is both the origin and the goal of everything that exists, including laughter. And when we demonstrate a "holy mirth," we give a positive witness that honors God, shows our acceptance and love of his creation, and gives evidence that the Christian way of life is really good and hopeful and joyous.

Chesterton once said that God's joy and laughter are just too much for humans to cope with here on earth. The Bible tells us that no one sees God and lives, and that suggests the question, What would happen if we were to experience the full explosion or radiation of God's comic spirit? If God's glory is too bright for human eyes, does he sometimes veil his comic spirit, something that would be much too funny for us to tolerate?

Although we know that God is fully and truly love and that he might compassionately restrain his humor for our good, he does not completely hide his laughter and comic spirit from us. We also know that from the biblical witness, our own experience, and revelation that God does indeed show us his sense of humor from time to time. He reveals this in many forms, including the funny ways he comes into our lives (usually unannounced), often quietly in those awkward moments when we least wish to be disturbed. He does this in the way he foils our selfish plans, only to answer our prayers beyond our wildest dreams. He does this in the way he insists on having the last laugh whenever we take something far too seriously or dismiss something far too lightly. He does this in the way he seems to play hide-and-seek with us, forever disturbing us as much by his presence as by his absence. And above all, God shows us his comic spirit by the way he does impossible things with impossible and improbable people; people whom we sometimes laugh at. Someone has said that this shows that God "writes straight with crooked lines," calling as his saints people who some of us wouldn't associate or even be seen with.

Yes, God does have a sense of humor and a comic

spirit, but we usually discover this through hindsight. Only when we look back on a particular event or circumstances do we become aware of God's humor and playfulness. The discovery is usually a delayed reaction, like when the disciples at Emmaus recognized the risen Lord only after he had traveled some distance with them. What prevents us from seeing God's comic spirit sooner? Our often-weak faith and spiritual obtuseness.

On the cover of its September 8, 1947, issue, *Time* pictured Lewis alongside a horned and tailed devil that bore a pitchfork. The magazine accused Lewis of being a heretic, but a different kind of heretic. His heresy, it was said, was being simply a witty mere Christian in a world that at that time needed it—and still does. It has since been discovered, contrary to what the movie *Shadowlands* portrayed, that Lewis did not live in a safe, isolated academic world free from pain. He had lost his mother when he was little boy; endured the horrors of the Great War; lost his father when he was in his thirties; lost his beloved wife after only a little more than three years of marriage; lived with an alcoholic brother; was never voted to an academic chair at Oxford due in large part to professional jealousy and opposition to his outspoken Christian faith; and was very ill the last years of his life.

Nevertheless, Lewis was a Christian who had a true comic spirit and loved to laugh. Thank goodness he was never spiritually obtuse! His comic spirit and knowledge of God's laughter can be seen in many of his famous works, particularly *The Screwtape Letters*, *The Great Divorce*, *Letters to Malcolm*, *Mere Christianity*, the Narnia tales, and several collections of letters. Although Lewis wrote about permanent things, serious topics like heaven, hell, the nature of evil, the problem of pain, grief, and others, he used humor and often a little bit of the ridiculous to make his serious topics more manageable for his readers. He also used humor because it was a natural way of expression for him. Lewis was a Christian who took God and life seriously, but because he took it seriously, he was able to see God's saving grace in his life. Lewis saw God working in him, working in the world, and working in the lives of countless others, and he was able to laugh and enjoy it.

It has been said that true humor is the knowledge of a fundamental discrepancy. The greatest discrepancy that can exist is the moral distance between the sinner and God. This moral distance, known in some circles as sin, perhaps is at its worst when we take ourselves too seriously, attribute too much honor to our own efforts, and give too much place to our own (often) self-righteous ideas and ideals. As an authentic and honest Christian, Lewis knew the reality of sin in his own life very well, and his laughter and comic spirit became a vehicle for bridging the gap between himself and God. He also used laughter and his comic gifts for another reason. Lewis possessed what the apostle Paul called "the peace of God that exceeds all understanding." That peace gave him a contented assurance that God does laugh—not at us, but with us and for us. As Christians, we can learn from the example of Lewis, and serve God with laughter and a comic spirit, a spirit that can smile in the good knowledge of his love.

30

Friendship

Spiritual Reading

It seems no wonder if our ancestors
regarded Friendship as something that
raised us almost above humanity. This
love, free from instinct, free from all
duties but those which love has freely
assumed, almost wholly free from
jealousy, and free without qualification
from the need to be needed, is
eminently spiritual. It is the sort of
love one can imagine between angels.

The Four Loves

On Friendship

Perry Bramlett

The Bible mentions two people who are called God's friends. In Exodus we are told that God spoke to Moses face-to-face, as one does with a friend, and the author of Isaiah tells us that God called Abraham his friend (echoed in James). We think about praying to God the Father, we are sometimes fearful of a God of judgment, in the best worship services we might think about an awesome and majestic God, and we are often told from pulpits that God is a loving God. But how often do we think of God as our friend? If we ponder the implications, that thought is almost too awesome to comprehend.

Jesus took the idea of friendship with God a step further (as he did about a lot of things), and we should keep in mind the fact that he told us that "whoever has seen me has seen the Father" (John 14:9). Late in his life, Jesus told his disciples that they had a chance to be his friends permanently if they would do what he commanded them. And his command to them was one of his most difficult: love each other. To be Jesus's friend, and thus God's friend, we have to be each other's friends, and we even have to be willing to sacrifice, Jesus said, and perhaps even die for the people we love.

Obviously, this is very important, and crucial for our development into mature Christians. If we can try to love and be friends with the people we know, we can actually be friends with God. In Christian tradition there is a relationship called "spiritual friendship," and it primarily concerns members of the same sex who shared a common faith and support each other in searching for God. Early Christians did use the words "friends of God" as a generic term referring to all Christians, but they did not call each other "friends," but rather "brethren." Spiritual friendship between both sexes was discouraged until the late 1600s, and now some Christian theologians see all true and lasting friendship as spiritual. Our love and friendship for others is founded on and encouraged by the love of God, and our love for God can be discerned or mirrored in our human friendships.

It is a bit disconcerting to discover that few modern, popular Christian writers have written about friendship that is spiritual. Writers like Martin Marty, Gilbert Meilaender, and Frederick Buechner come to mind, as does the great Methodist preacher Leslie Weatherhead, whose book *The Transforming Friendship* remains a classic model of an engaging, reader-friendly exposition of the reality of companionship with Jesus. But the most

Scripture

This is my commandment: love each other just as I have loved you. No one has greater love than to give up one's life for one's friends. You are my friends if you do what I command you. I don't call you servants any longer, because servants don't know what their master is doing. Instead, I call you friends, because everything I heard from my Father I have made known to you.

John 15:12-15

accessible words concerning spiritual friendship by a Christian writer who is read widely today came from the pen of C. S. Lewis. In works like *The Four Loves*, *Till We Have Faces*, and several collections of letters, Lewis wrote about friends and friendship in a way few ever have.

Lewis saw friendship differently than most and actually called it a form of love. For him, friendship (which might be described by the Greek word *philia*) was not just "fellowship," "companionship" (Lewis called this "clubbability"), or "being together." *Philia* is a deep, caring relationship based on common insights, interests, and tastes, and it should never be self-serving and "outwardly based." By this Lewis meant that real friendship, more often than not, involves a sharing of inward ideas and convictions, such as what a friend really believes about truth, faith, hope, and other ideals. Lewis believed that *companions* do outward things together, and true friends do also, but true friendship is about something; it has a common vision and hope and is often in the minority with other companions.

Lewis also believed that an important part of friendship is its "acceptability." A true friend never seeks or needs gratitude from the other and accepts the other simply as he or she is. Background, race, income, and status are not important, nor is discussing the nature of the friendship. Lewis wrote in *The Four Loves* that lovers always talk about their (romantic) love and are absorbed in each other, but true friends are absorbed in their common, inward interests.

For Lewis, the greatest barrier to real friendship was what he called corporate pride. This occurs when friends are indifferent to the opinions and ideas of others and therefore (at worst) become exclusive, arrogant, elitist, and even secretive. Lewis believed that when friends became exclusivist, they might ultimately turn into a coterie or clique. Such friendships have become a "self-appointed aristocracy," transformed from "individual humility" to corporate pride. Lewis said that friend groups like these have a sense of superiority that disdains and ignores those not in their circle.

Elsewhere Lewis called this group of friends an "inner ring" and reserved some of his strongest words for it. "Inner rings" are really power cliques, and the ambition to be a member of an in group could lead to the abuse of others, foster excess and selfish corporate pride, and break the rules of accepted morality and good behavior. Lewis wrote a famous essay called "The Inner Ring" and later wrote in *That Hideous Strength*, the last volume of his three famous space novels, a fictional account of this type of deadly friendship. In all of his writings about friendship, he stressed the point that the best friendships are those that are not exclusive or self-congratulatory, but that enjoy true friendship for what it is and what it can become, a gift from God that is spiritual.

Christian friendship is the highest of all friendships. Christian friends united by their common salvation should try to discover what is good and beautiful and true in each, and this is an instrument in which God reveals himself. Lewis saw this unity of Christian friends as an integral part of the church universal; the very survival of the church depends on God-centered relationships. Lewis knew that little pockets of Christians survived and flourished because they cared for each other with a spiritual, giving, non-exclusive friendship. Because he believed this, Lewis saw his good friends as friends for life and saw this as one of the best things on this earth that Christianity offers.

Lewis's best friends were called the Inklings, and this group met regularly from around 1933 through the early 1950s. The Inklings most often met on Tuesdays for lunch at the Eagle and Child pub in Oxford, and on Thursday evenings at Lewis's rooms at Magdalen College. The Inklings were an informal group that had no rules or agenda. Members varied through the years, but most were friends of Lewis, including J. R. R. Tolkien; the writer and poet Charles Williams; Lewis's brother, Warren; and others, mostly professors. They would discuss politics, the books they were reading and writing, religion, and some of their shared interests and concerns. Lewis read *The Screwtape Letters*, *The Problem of Pain*, *The Great Divorce*, and other works to the group, and Tolkien read to them parts of *The Hobbit* and *The Lord of the Rings*.

One of the great attributes of the Inklings was that the group was not a mutual admiration society, which many so-called reading or support groups are today.

These friends and colleagues respected and cared for one another, but criticism and opinions were honest and frank. The Inklings relied on one another for support and encouragement and became one of the most famous Christian literary groups. One member, commenting about the meetings, said that, at their best, they were as good as anything he would ever live to see.

If Christians today are going to commit themselves to fostering spiritual friendships, they can learn from Lewis and his friends that friendship must be a priority. In our busy, not-enough-time and too-much-work culture, many Christians fail to make time to be with each other in friendship, even at church. There are too many acquaintances and not enough real friends. We often try to gloss this over by using terms like *work friend*, *tennis friend*, and the like, when we really mean *acquaintance*. We live in a world where work and vocation dominate, and many of us identify ourselves (and others) in terms of what we do for pay and where we live, not by who our friends are and how much time we spend with them.

A modern author has added the modifier *preferential* to the word *friendship*, and he is right on the mark. Friendship should be a preferred activity. When we love and honor our friends as God does us, we are enriched personally and spiritually and we can know that this also gives God pleasure. In a great scene from the movie *Chariots of Fire*, the future Olympic runner Eric Liddell tries to explain to his sister why he *has* to run, rather than return to the mission field. He tells her, in one of the most memorable lines from any movie, "When I run, I feel God's pleasure." The good news is that God does take pleasure in us, and when we honor and cultivate our human friendships, we can truly become God's friend and know that pleasure.

Acknowledgments

We are deeply grateful for those who have labored to preserve the significant work of C. S. Lewis. To have this treasure for this and future generations is an enormous gift to all who seek to more fully understand what it means to be human and what it means to be Christian. Lewis was a superb defender and embodiment of mere Christianity, and it is our hope and prayer that this volume will inspire others who seek to practice their faith with integrity and trust.

We are also grateful for our readers, who seek a growing, vibrant, and trustful relationship with God that results in lives of integrity as they practice "mere Christianity" where they live. They are the ones who make the world more sane, peaceful, equitable, and loving—as we believe God intends.

Perry Bramlett
Rueben P. Job
Norman Shawchuck

Notes

Salvation

C. S. Lewis, *Mere Christianity* (New York: Macmillan, 1977), 138.

Joy

Clyde S. Kilby, ed., *A Mind Awake: An Anthology of C. S. Lewis* (New York: Harcourt, Brace and Co., 1968), 26.

Serenity

C. S. Lewis, *The Problem of Pain* (New York: HarperCollins, 2001), 152–53.

Prayer

Lewis, *Mere Christianity* (1977), 131.

The Trinity

Lewis, *Mere Christianity* (1977), 127.

C. S. Lewis, *Letters of C. S. Lewis*, ed. W. H. Lewis (New York: Harcourt, Brace & Co., 1988), 382.

C. S. Lewis, *Christian Reflections*, ed. Walter Hooper (Grand Rapids: Eerdmans, 1995), 79–80.

Worship

C. S. Lewis, *The Weight of Glory and Other Addresses* (New York: HarperCollins, 2001), 158.

God

C. S. Lewis, *Miracles: A Preliminary Study* (New York: Simon and Schuster, 1996), 121.

Evil

C. S. Lewis, *Christian Reflections* (Grand Rapids: Eerdmans, 1955), 33.

The Bible

Lewis, *Letters of C. S. Lewis* (1988), 428.

Devotional Life

C. S. Lewis, *Reflections on the Psalms* (New York: Harcourt, Brace & Co., 1986), 111–12.

Sin

C. S. Lewis, *The Problem of Pain* (San Francisco: Harper-SanFrancisco, 1996), 55.

Christian Marriage

Lewis, *Letters of C. S. Lewis* (1988), 347–48.
C. S. Lewis, *A Grief Observed* (London: Faber and Faber, 1961), 42.

Jesus

C. S. Lewis, "What Are We to Make of Jesus Christ?" in *God in the Dock: Essays on Theology and Ethics* (Grand Rapids: Eerdmans, 2002), 160.

Running from God

Lewis, *The Problem of Pain* (2001), 119.

Conversion

Lewis, "The Decline of Religion," in *God in the Dock*, 221.

The Risk of Discipleship

C. S. Lewis, *Mere Christianity* (New York: HarperCollins, 2001), 207.

Grief

Lewis, *A Grief Observed*, 5.

Faith

C. S. Lewis, "On Obstinacy in Belief," in *The World's Last Night and Other Essays* (New York: Harcourt Brace Jovanovich, 1960), 26.

The Holy Spirit

C. S. Lewis, *The Chronicles of Narnia, Book I: The Magician's Nephew* (New York: HarperCollins, 2000), 125–26.

Forgiveness

C. S. Lewis, *Letters to an American Lady*, ed. Clyde S. Kilby (Grand Rapids: Eerdmans, 1967), 82.

Aslan's Country

C. S. Lewis, *The Chronicles of Narnia, Book II: The Lion, the Witch, and the Wardrobe* (New York: HarperCollins, 2000), 78–79.

Hope of Heaven

Lewis, *Miracles: A Preliminary Study*, 256.

Spirituality in Nature

Lewis, *Miracles: A Preliminary Study*, 214.

The Heart of a Child

C. S. Lewis, *A Mind Awake: An Anthology of C. S. Lewis* (Boston: Houghton Mifflin, 2003), 246.

C. S. Lewis, *Letters to Children* (New York: Simon and Schuster, 1995), 28.

Lewis, *Letters to Children*, 97.

The Church and Sacraments

C. S. Lewis, *Reflections on the Psalms* (New York: Harcourt, Brace & Co., 1958), 52.

Evangelism

C. S. Lewis, *Letters of C. S. Lewis*, ed. W. H. Lewis (New York: Harcourt, Brace & Co., 1993), 428.

The Grace of Good Books

C. S. Lewis, *An Experiment in Criticism* (Cambridge, UK: Cambridge University Press, 1961), 140–41.

Spiritual Direction

C. S. Lewis, *Letters to an American Lady*, ed. Clyde S. Kilby (Grand Rapids: Eerdmans, 1971), 111, 112.

Laughter and the Comic Spirit

Lewis, *The Weight of Glory and Other Addresses*, 46.

Friendship

C. S. Lewis, *The Four Loves* (New York: Harcourt Brace Jovanovich, 1988), 77.

About the Authors

Perry Bramlett (1945–2013), a pastor, founded C. S. Lewis for the Local Church—Interstate Ministries, a nationwide speaking ministry on the life, works, and influence of C. S. Lewis. He wrote several books about Lewis's life and influence, including *C. S. Lewis: Life at the Centre* and *Touring C. S. Lewis' Ireland and England: A Travel Guide to C. S. Lewis' Favourite Places to Walk and Visit.*

Rueben P. Job (1928–2015) was a United Methodist bishop, pastor, and acclaimed author and served as World Editor of The Upper Room publishing program. Best-known for his classic book *Three Simple Rules: A Wesleyan Way of Living,* he also authored or coauthored spiritual works such as *A Guide to Prayer for Ministers and Other Servants; A Wesleyan Spiritual Reader; Living Fully, Dying Well;* and *Listen: Praying in a Noisy World.* He also co-edited *Finding Our Way: Love and Law in The United Methodist Church.* Bishop Job also chaired the Hymnal Revision Committee that developed the 1989 *United Methodist Hymnal.*

Norman Shawchuck (1935–2012) was ordained in The United Methodist Church and served as a pastor and seminary professor. He wrote several books about the practice of congregational ministry and coauthored, with Rueben Job, *A Guide to Prayer for Ministers and Other Servants, A Guide to Prayer for All Who Seek God,* and *A Guide for Prayer for All God's People.*